MW00364096

STAIRWAY TO HEAVEN

The Psalms of Ascent (120-134) and the Spiritual Life

STAIRWAY
to
HEAVEN

The Psalms of Ascent (120–134)
and the Spiritual Life

WILLIAM R. LONG, M Div, Ph D, JD

STERLING REED
BOOKS

Copyright © 2020 by William R. Long

Cover and interior design by Masha Shubin
Cover Image: "Jacob's Dream" by Gustave Doré's from *La Grande Bible de Tours* 1866

All rights reserved. No part of this book may be reproduced or transmitted in any form or by any means whatsoever, including photocopying, recording or by any information storage and retrieval system, without written permission from the publisher and/or author.

New Revised Standard Version Bible, copyright © 1989 National Council of the Churches of Christ in the United States of America. Used by permission. All rights reserved.

Publisher: Stirling Reed Books

ISBN 978-1-7350927-2-0

1 3 5 7 9 10 8 6 4 2

Contents

Foreword

T HE IDEA FOR THIS BOOK EMERGED DURING A LONG PERIOD OF CRE-
ative fervor in the summer and fall of 2018. That period saw
both the germ and fruition of many ideas. Some of those Ideas
have already seen the light of day as books, such as my book
on Chinese love poetry (with Eurydice Chen) and my study of
the Book of Job. Several more books have already been written
and are awaiting my patient editing to bring them to publication,
either in book or website form (www.drbilllong.com). Among
them are a lengthy commentary on Job, a reflection on Psalm
119, an exploration into the Bible's bleakest Psalm (88), a commentary on Genesis, a very long introduction to Confucius for
Western readers, a small book on the Book of Jonah, a brief trea-
tise on learning, and my autobiography.

An important partner in placing these ideas in an attractive
format has been Inkwater Press in Portland OR. Whether it is the
warm welcome and efficient work of Sean Jones, the design bril-
liance of Masha Shubin or the author support of Vanessa Verrill,
Inkwater has repeatedly shown itself able to take my sometimes
jumbled thoughts and put them in an appealing and accessible
form. I will forever be grateful for their cheerful spirit and pub-
lishing skill.

Salem OR
March 2020

Introduction

THE PSALMS OF ASCENT IS A COLLECTION OF 15 SHORT SONGS (Psalms 120-134) whose total length barely exceeds half the length of the single longest Psalm (Psalm 119), which directly precedes it. One can look at the messages of Psalm 119 and Psalms 120-134 as mutually reinforcing or supporting each other. Psalm 119 treats of the wonders of the Law of God, the obedience to which was the foundational principle of Israelite religion while Psalms 120-134 deal with the joys and struggles of the journey to Jerusalem to participate in festivals of the people of God.

Psalm 119 roots us in faith; Psalms 120-134 give us direction in living out that faith. Psalm 119 leads to mental affirmations or beliefs; Psalms 120-134 bring us to the practice of religion. Psalm 119, for all its robust language and explosive power, is a quintessentially interior Psalm, for it directs us to the process of learning and mastery, while Psalms 120-134 lead us to participate in the lives of the people of God. Psalm 119 starts with delight in the law of God; Psalm 134 ends with a blessing on those who have experienced the unity of the people of God described in Psalm 133.

In this book my sole focus will be on the Psalms of Ascent. Ever since they appeared together under the common title of "Songs of Ascent" (*shir hammaloth*) faithful readers have advanced numerous theories as to what one might call the social or religious function of these songs. Of the seven or eight theories suggested, the four most prominent are:

1. These Psalms were sung by exiles returning after the Babylonian captivity in the mid sixth-century BCE, with the reference to dangers of rivers (Psalm 124:4) or restoration of

fortunes (Psalm 126) suggestive of the joyous, though per-
ilous, return of the exiles to Jerusalem.

2. These Psalms were sung by the Levites on the fifteen-step
    staircase leading from the Court of the Women to the Court
    of the Israelites in the Jerusalem Temple. This theory reads
    the word "ascent" as referring to a "staircase" (the word is
    so used in Ezek 40:6). Two passages in the Mishnah, a 3rd
    century CE sacred Jewish book, make reference to the Levites
    singing these Psalms on the fifteen steps between the Court
    of the Women and the Court of the Israelites in Jerusalem.
    Many Jewish and Christian interpreters, including Martin
    Luther, have adopted this theory.

3. These Psalms simply reflect musical directions to singers. This
    theory eschews any connection between these Psalms and his-
    torical or specific liturgical events and simply argues that the
    frequent repetition in the songs suggests the rising notes in
    which subsequent verses were intoned. The song thus "ascended"
    or "rose" in tone or pitch from the first to the last verse.

4. These songs were sung by religious pilgrims in their journeys
    from their local tribal locations to Jerusalem to celebrate one
    of the three annual festivals of the people (Passover/Unleav-
    ened Bread, Pentecost/Weeks and Tabernacles/Booths). As
    the Scriptures say, "Three times a year all your males shall
    appear before the Lord your God at the place that he will
    choose: at the festival of unleavened bread, at the festival of
    weeks, and at the festival of booths. They shall not appear
    before the Lord empty-handed" (Deut 16:16). The movement
    "up" suggests, as any who has visited Israel can attest, the
    need to ascend sometimes steep hills to get to Jerusalem; the
    frequent antiphonal calls in these Psalms are suggestive of
    pilgrims calling to each other to lend encouragement and sup-
    port on the arduous climb.

My Approach

Though no theory has gained universal support, the majority
of scholars in our day would probably be most sympathetic to
the fourth. As I will argue below, the structure of the Psalms of
Ascent also makes considerable sense in describing the nature of
the spiritual life. There is a long tradition of seeing our spiritual
life as a journey from isolation or the margins of life to the center
of life, which is presented here as the Holy City or Jerusalem. In
other words, I take these Psalms as standing, metaphorically, for
the spiritual journey we make from our isolation or the margins
of our own existence to the presence of God and to unity with
the people of God. That this journey was only to be undertaken
by men in antiquity should not deter us from applying its message to any who truly seek that spiritual journey today.

The goal of the pilgrimages spoken of in Deuteronomy was
for the people of God to experience its unity as a people and to
renew its covenant publicly with God. With a strengthened sense
of national identify and religious unity, the men would return to
their locations. Rooted thus in a common covenant, a common law
and a common sense of fellowship, the people of God maintained
an identity which continues in a sturdy and healthy form today.

The Psalms of Ascent capture the danger, anticipation, joy,
longing, sadness and unity of the people of God as they go on
a journey to Jerusalem and as they settle in for the festivals.
Because Jerusalem is higher in elevation than most of the surrounding countryside, the movement to Jerusalem is "up." People
are "climbing to Zion" and singing these songs as they go. These
Psalms, then, are their Stairway to Heaven. We will find, curi-
ously at first, that the pilgrims reach the very gates of Jerusalem
quite early in the journey (Psalm 122) leaving 12 Psalms to
describe what you might call "life in Jerusalem." And that reality
provides an interesting insight into the life of faith. Any who see
the spiritual life as a sort of journey or quest know that there
was a time, perhaps in the distant past, where they were squarely

standing at the gates of Jerusalem. They had arrived at their destination. But there was still so much life to be lived! Though the spiritual life may aptly be characterized as a journey, most of it actually takes place within the confines of Jerusalem, the locus of salvation and the people of God. Being in Jerusalem, therefore, doesn't end life. If anything, it gives new direction and focus to the spiritual quest and yearning. Thus, the journey to Jerusalem or the Stairway to Heaven doesn't end with first arrival; the quest for God, for insight, for unity and for meaning take on new depth once we have entered the Holy City.

But we have to start our journey somewhere. That is why we are grateful that Psalm 120, an otherwise unprepossessing Psalm, initiates our trip. As we turn to it, we will see that our journey to Jerusalem, that long and arduous climb, only makes sense if we see ourselves at first as living in a place far removed from Jerusalem, far away from the sources of comfort and meaning that a living faith provides. So, let's begin the journey. We don't saddle up a horse or call an Uber or Lyft. We are on foot.

Two final notes. The cover image for this book is entitled "Jacob's Dream," from Gustave Doré's (1832-1883) illustrations for the *La Grande Bible de Tours* of 1866. Doré's images became wildly popular and have frequently been reproduced in many contexts. The cover of this book illustrates the scene in the Book of Genesis where Jacob falls asleep and sees angels of God ascending and descending a stairway to heaven (Genesis 28). The cover contains about half of the image. The depiction is especially appropriate for this book not simply because it shows the image of the stairway, but because it suggests that this stairway is flanked by angels. Genesis 28 mentions angels; Psalms 120-134 do not. But by having Doré's woodcut on the cover, the reader is encouraged to consider how Psalms 120-134 might be read in their larger Scriptural context. No angels are mentioned in Psalms 120-134, but who is to say that our stairway isn't also lined by them?

Finally, my method here is to provide the English text of each Psalm of Ascent from the New Revised Standard Version, then provide what I call the "Psalm in a Nutshell," and finally go verse by verse in expositing its meaning. Each verse or portion of verse that I interpret will first be given in my more literal translation of the Hebrew, placed in quotation marks. The following exposition will focus on the meaning of the language and my own observations on the text. My hope is that you will not only appreciate more deeply the relevance of this collection of Psalms to your own journey of faith but will see that the language in which faith is expressed is worth taking the time to study closely.

Summary of This Book's Contents

From one perspective the thesis of this book is rather unexceptional—that the Psalms of Ascent present the songs sung by pilgrims on their thrice-annual, Scripturally-commanded, visits to the Holy City. On another level, however, at least two things set this book apart from others on the same subject. First, I try to point out how the movements of the Psalms of Ascent powerfully and precisely reflect movements in the spiritual life for those who have made their personal journey of faith (a "Journey to Jerusalem") or, in the language of this book, have climbed the Stairway to Heaven. Second, I have paid close attention to the actual words used to describe this journey and, through these words, have often been led to other portions of Scripture for further illumination of the journey and its nature. Thus, I claim that there is movement or direction in these Psalms, just as one might characterize one's own life as a journey along a path.

As a result, I favor a synoptic rather than an atomistic reading of these Psalms. Of course there are many who might say, "Psalm 121 is simply my favorite Psalm," and I would have no quarrel with that. A journey is not only beautiful for the movement of it but for the power of the photos taken along the way that freeze the action. Further, by focusing on the precise words that describe the contours of this journey to and life in Jerusalem, we are forced to slow down and, in the words of another Psalm, "Walk about Zion, go all around it, count its towers, consider well its ramparts, go through its citadels. . ." (Ps 48:12-13). Precision in examination and expression is an ally for those who walk the path of faith. The Scriptures themselves invite and reward that close consideration of words.

Yet it is viewing these Psalms as a whole that motivates this book. The major points of the journey of faith, derived from these Psalms and presented in this book are these. First, our journey of faith usually begins with a feeling of being distant or far away from the center of our life, even to the extent of living in an enervating and harmful environment (Psalm 120). Sometimes, even in the life of faith, that feeling never really leaves us. Solitude, even angry and frustrating solitude, may accompany us longer than we thought it might. Second, the journey begins (Psalm 121). It has its rhythmic and exhilarating dimensions and, sooner than expected, we make it to Jerusalem. We settle in (Psalm 122), look around, and are filled with the joy of the newly-arrived. But then, distress enters (Psalm 123). Distress enters because the memories from the past keep nagging us. Those who treated us with contempt back in Meshech and Kedar (Psalm 120) continue to do so—at least in our dreams or our flashbacks. We no doubt think of witty responses we wish we had delivered to them; we think of clever ways to give them what they really deserved. But our souls become "fully sated" with the scorn of those we thought we had discarded. Only in Psalm 124 do we arrive at a place of personal comfort and harmony. It is as if, in the words of TS Eliot's memorable *Journey of the Magi*, after "a hard time we had of it,"

> "Then at dawn we came down to a temperate valley,
> Wet, below the snow line, smelling of vegetation;
> With a running stream and a water-mill beating the darkness."

The Psalms of Ascent continue to take us on a well-crafted

and psychologically sensitive journey through several more stages of the spiritual life. And not every step is a glorious one. In addition to those just mentioned, we have the following: stability (Psalm 124), satisfaction (Psalm 125), joy (Psalm 126), fruitfulness (Psalm 127), blessedness or uber-fruitfulness (Psalm 128), seeking of retaliation (Psalm 129), plunging into the depths (Psalm 130), humility (Psalm 131), memory (Psalm 132), unity (Psalm 133) and blessing (Psalm 134). The new life of faith keeps opening up larger and larger circles of insight and pleasure. Yet we would be untrue to ourselves and to the Scriptures if we tried to remove the elements of seeming retreat from blessedness as we explore recurrent desires for retaliation and the subsequent plunge into the depths. Perhaps after remerging from the depths of Psalm 130 we can learn to say with the Psalmist, "Even the darkness isn't dark to you; the night is as bright as the day" (Psalm 139:12).

As I think of the flow of this book, I almost envision someone coming up with a kind of Psalms of Ascent game or, even better, a "Psalms of Ascent wheel," whose needle points to one of the ten or twelve movements of the spiritual life according to those laid out in this book. One could "spin the Psalms of Ascent wheel" and then, wherever it lands, one would be required to narrate a time in one's life which matches where the needle landed. Thus, if one spun and it came to "Psalm 124" or "stability," a story would have to come about a time when one felt a deep sense of personal security and stability in life. And, if one couldn't come up with one, then one goes back to Meshech and Kedar in Psalm 120! In an amusing sort of way, such a task might get one to think more deeply and purposefully about the movements of our spiritual lives, both in distress and joy.

The final word of the book however, will belong to joy or blessedness. Just as the night-serving Levites gave us the final word of these Psalms, anchoring their blessing in the "Lord who made heaven and earth" (Psalm 134:3), so I take leave of this task with the hope that your days in these Psalms will be blessed, that you will deepen yourself in each movement that it narrates to the end that you may articulately tell your story and lead others to recognize and tell theirs. Then we will have a chance to celebrate some of the oil-flowing-down-the-beard unity of Psalm 133, the joy of the harvest of Psalm 126, the quiet confidence that pervades many of these Psalms. We will be able joyfully to recite our own Journey to Jerusalem, our own Stairway to Heaven, and the rich contours of life in the Holy City.

STAIRWAY TO HEAVEN

The Psalms of Ascent (120-134) and the Spiritual Life

Psalm 120 A Song of Ascents

1 In my distress I cry to the Lord,
    that he may answer me:
2 'Deliver me, O Lord,
    from lying lips,
    from a deceitful tongue.'

3 What shall be given to you?
    And what more shall be done to you,
    you deceitful tongue?
4 A warrior's sharp arrows,
    with glowing coals of the broom tree!

5 Woe is me, that I am an alien in Meshech,
    that I must live among the tents of Kedar.
6 Too long have I had my dwelling
    among those who hate peace.
7 I am for peace;
    but when I speak,
    they are for war.

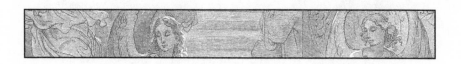

Psalm 120 in a Nutshell

This Psalm, the first of the Psalms of Ascent, describes the beginning of one's spiritual quest. Though the goal for the Psalmist will be to arrive at Jerusalem, the center of the spiritual life, the quest begins far from that center. One might characterize the beginning point alliteratively as the "margins of Mechech" or the "caves of Kedar" (see v 5). That is, one often begins the quest at a distance from the ultimate goal. Though the concept of distance may have a spatial dimension to it, as it does here, it is primarily a recognition of a gap, yawning or narrow, between one's comfort in a present situation and one's longing for something better. Often, as in Psalm 120, the motivation to embark on the path of the spiritual life comes from dissatisfaction with one's current condition—one has to endure the "deceitful tongues" or murmurings of those who "hate peace." But sooner or later, one says to oneself, 'I want to change my life and my orientation to it. I am going on pilgrimage.' That decision initiates a journey of immense importance, challenge, difficulty and joy. Psalm 120 presents the time before that journey begins.

1 "A song of going up. To the Lord, in distress to me, I called and He answered me"

We only have eight Hebrew words in this verse, but they bring us immediately into a specific aspect of human life—the world of distress. The first two Hebrew words are the superscription or title, and this same title will begin each of these 15 Psalms. We are "going up" (the noun *ma'alah,* ascent, is derived from the common Hebrew verb for ascending or going up, *alah)* in them all. But in this Psalm we begin not on the hill but in distant places. The structure of the opening verse is a bit unusual, and I try to capture it in my translation. Distress is the concept smack in the middle of the verse (expressed by the two Hebrew words "distress to me"—*tsarathah liy*—rather than the one Hebrew word "my distress"), surrounded by God and calling/answer. If we were to eliminate the superscription, thus leaving the verses with six words, the "distress to me" are words three and four of six. Literarily, then, we might say that God envelops the distress or anguish and removes it, yet the felt experience of any in distress it that it is middle or center of our lives. Distress is *tsarah* (the word appears 73x in the Bible) which can be variously translated as "troubles" or "distress" or even a "rival' or "adversary." The verbs in the verse are common ones for calling and answering (*qara/anah).* They appear in the past tense, suggesting that this verse is a kind of statement of faith derived from experience. God has delivered in the past, which gives the Psalmist hope that in his present condition God will also be sufficient for the task.

In structure and meaning, the six words of Psalm 120:1 after the superscription are very close to those of Psalm 34:6, "This poor man cried and the Lord heard, and saved him from all his distress." Note how the conceptual worlds of Psalm 120:1 and Psalm 34:6 completely overlap while the linguistic choices only partially intersect. We have the concepts of distress, call, and delivery in both. Same structure. Yet, the only three shared words are "distress/trouble/anxiety/anguish" (*tsarah*), "call/cry" (*qara),* and

4

"Lord" (*yaveh*). Whereas Psalm 120 talks about "I" and "Lord" and "calling" and "distress" and "answering", Psalm 34 speaks of this "poor/afflicted/humble man" (*ani*) and "Lord" and "calling" and "hearing" (*shema*) and "distress" and "saving" (*yasha*). Thus, we have about eight or nine useful Hebrew words to begin to capture one aspect of our experience of faith. We begin our journey of building Hebrew vocabulary, if that also is your interest, by studying identical thought patterns and realizing the freedom and joy in selecting slightly different words to describe that similar reality. By paying close attention to linguistic choices we become aware of our own modes of communication and strive to capture with precision and power exactly what we want to describe.

As mentioned, the word for distress (*tsarah*) appears 73 times in the Bible, with almost a third of them (24) in the Psalms. While many scholars talk of the Psalms as "Israel's Book of Praise," a more apt title might be "Israel's Distress Book." The Book of Psalms, like no other book, understands what you might call the full scope of distress—how you get there, what it is, how it continues, how to deal with it, what it feels like to wallow in it, etc. If you are in trouble, if anxiety rips at you, if distress overwhelms, then the Psalms should be the first place to turn. The Psalmist turned to God in his trouble in the past, and was delivered. Thus the implicit question of the verse, 'Is God up to handling this *current* trouble?

2 "Oh Lord, deliver my soul from lying lips and from a deceitful tongue"

If verse 1 was a confident confession of past deliverance, verse 2 takes us into the Psalmist's new distress. At present he seems surrounded not by the love and care of an answering God but by lips spewing out their polluted flow of poisonous and deceptive filth. It is as if the Psalmist is like a person today who might say to a friend, "Yeah, I trust in God and I have seen God work in my life, but this time I am really facing something that may be more than

I can handle." When an Israelite fell into distress and called upon God, four words that were useful to capture what the petitioner wanted are "hear" (*shema*), "answer" (*anah*), "save" (*yasha*), and "deliver" (*natsal*). Our Psalmist selects the verbs for "answer" in verse 1 and the "deliver" in verse 2. The verb "to deliver" (*natsal*) appears more than 200 times in the Bible; its most vivid early biblical usage occurs in the Joseph narrative of Genesis, where Reuben "rescued" his brother Joseph out of the clutches of the other brothers (Genesis 37:21). Of course, Reuben's motives weren't altogether pure, but that is beyond our scope here. By doing our quick vocabulary work, then, we see that the Psalmist asks for deliverance in 120:2 in a standard, though heartfelt, way. Rather than describing his current trouble as being assailed by evildoers (Psalm 27) or tumbling into a miry pit (Psalms 40; 69), he is mired in a different kind of conundrum—that of lying and deceitful words.

We might do well to pause for a moment and consider the corrosive effect of hateful or deceitful words on one's motivation to thrive. Though most of us grew up on the common American saw, "Sticks and stones can break my bones, but words can never hurt me," that adage is almost certainly false. Words hurt. In fact, the two biblical images that capture the injurious nature of words are that of arrows (later in this Psalm) and a fire (James 3). Arrows tear and fires singe. Arrows rend; fires incinerate. We don't know the specifics of the Psalmist's complaint about the deceptive words, and we don't need to ("Mr XXX said XXX of me"), but we can easily understand how hurtful words can leave a person feeling utterly undone.

The Scriptures are full of lines registering the caustic, abrasive and escharotic effect of words. Two examples will suffice. "For I have heard the slander of many, terror is on every side. They take counsel together against me, they schemed to take away my life" (Psalm 31:13). Jeremiah said, echoing these thoughts, "I hear whispering of many, 'Terror on every side! Denounce him; yes let us denounce him" (20:11). Harmful words can leave a scar as deep as any knife plunged into the body. If you ask people about good and bad influences on them, note how they speak. The majority will likely say that it was the *words* of someone, rather than their actions, that left the deepest impression. In this case, we have the common Hebrew device of parallelism to capture these words. Literally it is "lips lying, tongue deceptive." Parallelism is great—it doubles your vocabulary in one thought, or, colloquially speaking, you get the second word free when you buy the first at full price. As for the four words in parallelism in verse 2, only *remiyyah*, "deception" or "treachery," appears relatively infrequently (15 occurrences). Hebrew has a whole panoply of words to describe deception, but most of them seem to swirl around the same Hebrew verb, whose root is *ramah.* The two noun forms derived from this are *mirmah* and *remiyyah.* Close examination of the six dozen or so appearances of these three words in the Bible would give us a full-orbed treatment of aspects of betrayal, cheating, deception, beguilement. Suffice it to say for our purposes that the author of Psalm 120 is suffering under the effects of deceptive words.

An interpretation that would be permitted from the grammar of verse 2 alone is that the *Psalmist himself* may be the source of the deceptive words. One, then, might read verse two as an exasperated address of the self to the self, a self which has perhaps compromised too long with and participated in ways of speaking and acting that are harmful. If this is the case, the author would be chiding himself, encouraging himself to change harmful behavior. In either case, a change is in the offing.

3 "What shall be given to you, what shall be added to you, deceptive tongue?"

The Psalmist is in a sorry state. He is oppressed, battered, overwhelmed, crushed, beaten down by these deceptive words, whether they originate from others or from himself. Rather than internalize the thoughts and perhaps end up plunging into depths of self-pity or self-hatred, the Psalmist directs his thoughts outward. He uses words that echo a formula known in the Scriptures as a "curse formula" or at least the prelude to such a curse. It runs something like: "God do to you and add more to you if you don't xxxxx. . ." Eli said such a phrase to little Samuel (I Sam 3:17) in a memorable verse: "God do so to you and add even more if you don't tell me the word which was spoken to you" (triple use of *dabar,* "word"). Ps 120:3 functions as a prelude to the Psalmist's expression of his desire for judgment against those who have harassed him so bitterly with their deceptive tongues or against his own tongue. Finally, note the doubling of the last phrase in verse 3: *lashon remiyyah,* or "deceptive tongue." It is the same phrase that ended verse 2. That the Psalmist repeats the words indicates he has been 'burned' or 'sliced' pretty badly by words.

Repetition of words will be a common device in the Psalms of Ascent. This device almost functions as repeated "steps" on the rocky climb up a hill. You take a step, a short one, and sometimes slip back, needing to repeat your step. Thus, the repetition of words can be done either for emphasis or as a reflection of the reality of the arduous climb to Jerusalem.

4 "Arrows of the mighty, sharpened, along with coals of juniper!"

This verse is a cipher. The thought, unusually and allusively expressed, is perhaps best read as the Psalmist's hope for himself in this situation—that God would pierce the deceitful tongue with the arrows of judgment. This interpretation suggests that the "mighty" (the common *gibbor)* is none other than God, who will now string the divine bow and shoot. The "sharpened" arrows are expressed through the passive participle of the verb *shanan,* "to whet/sharpen." Read in this way, the first phrase presages divine judgment against those of lying and deceitful lips.

Yet this interpretation is far from certain. We might also see the "sharpened arrows" of the "mighty" as identical to the lying or deceitful lips of the preceding verses. After all, in a phrase using the same, rare verb for "sharpen/whet" (*shanan*) as in 120:4 and the same word for "tongue" in 120:2, we have the Psalmist pleading for deliverance (*natsal*, the same verb as in 120:2) from enemies who have "sharpened their tongues" (Ps 140:2, 4). In this reading, then, the "arrows of the mighty" might be a metaphorical reference to the sharpened tongues of those mentioned in verses 2-3. We see an inviting, though somewhat bewildering, array of possibilities for reading this phrase.

But what might the phrase "with coals of broom/juniper" mean? The second half of the verse most likely further describes these arrows (i.e., "warmed up"), which are ready for their target. Judgment, thus, is being "warmed up" for the deceitful tongue. Yet, even though it is expressed this way, it isn't the kind of malediction, execration, imprecation, hex or jinx (see how blessed English is with sophisticated words for cursing?) that easily flows from the mouth of twenty-first century readers. We may utter some kind of curse in high dudgeon or, more likely, think of a curse on someone, but the language is a bit too strong for us.

Yet just like everything else, curses have their history and their usual contexts of utterance. In a traditional agricultural setting, a curse such as "may your horses grow lame" or "may your cows go dry" gets at the nub of it. Curses in fairy tales, in addition, are different than curses in real life. A more fruitful comparison to illumine our passage comes not from other "curse passages" but from a passage describing the imminent judgment on the people of God—Jeremiah 9. In that passage Jeremiah explores concepts that are front and center in Psalm 120, such as dwelling with the wrong people, deception, treacherous speech, arrows and judgment.

Jeremiah was heartbroken by the obduracy of his people, people who had heard about God's judgment on the northern tribes a century earlier and now see the the Babylonian troops encircling Jerusalem. Though seeing this situation, they seemingly don't take the danger to heart. They either continue to live blissfully unaware of the danger or they backbite and slander, eroding further any notion of community. So, in Jeremiah 9, the prophet longs to escape ("Oh that I were in the wilderness, in a lodging-place for wayfarers"—9:1 (Hebrew)/9:2 (English); the rest of the citations are from the English), a sentiment remarkably similar to what the Psalmist will utter in the next verse. Jeremiah describes his contemporaries in words that our Psalmist could have used: "They bend their tongues, their bow of falsehood" and "proceed from evil to evil" (9:3). Then, using two of the four words in the parallelism of Psalm 120:2, Jeremiah continues: "they have taught their tongue (*lashon*) to speak lies (*sheqer*, 9:5)." Then, as if on cue, Jeremiah picks up on the theme of deception or treachery in 9:5, "Your habitation is in the midst of deceit" (*bethok mirmah*), using the linguistically similar word to *remiyyah* in Psalm 120:3. Then, as if to remove all doubt that these two passages occupy the same mental space, and perhaps drew up on each other, Jeremiah says, "Their tongue is a sharpened arrow" (*chets shachut leshonam*, 9:8), where the same word for arrow is used but a different word for "sharpened." Though normally translated "sharpen" or "whet" or "pierce," the most striking appearance of the verb in Psalm 120:4, *shanan*, is its first appearance in the famous recitation of Deuteronomy 6:7, where the phrase "you shall teach them (the commandments) diligently" is literally, "you shall pierce them diligently/sharpen them diligently. . ."

But what is the result that Jeremiah contemplates? Like the Psalmist here, Jeremiah envisions divine judgment: "Shall I not punish them for this? \ Shall not my soul be avenged on such a nation as this?" (9:9). The structural overlap between the two is almost identical. In fact, one might imagine the Psalmist taking Jeremiah as his "model" in framing his thoughts on isolation, deceit, arrows and judgment. The only new thought that the Psalmist adds is the "coals of the juniper," which suggests a sort of continuous flow of the arrows, since new arrowheads are heated and pounded into shape through fires produced by the coal-producing juniper. Readers have often had lots of problems with the "judgmental" or "sub-Christian" attitude expressed by the Psalmist in this verse but if put in the context of Jeremiah 9 we see this as a sort of oracle of judgment, very familiar to the prophets of Israel. No one seems to have problems with Jeremiah speaking about imminent judgment on the people of God—why should there be a ruckus over the Psalmist uttering similar thoughts against slanderers or the wicked tongue? When you have been assailed by vicious rumors or debilitating verbal attacks, you simply cannot shift into the forgiveness mode. You are hurt and you feel, and usually express, your desire for judgment. But when many ethically-oriented people express a desire for judgment on others, it is immediately followed by feelings of remorse or self-pity. That is what happens in this Psalm, too, in the next verse.

5 "Woe to me, that I make a temporary stay/sojourn in Meshech, that I am settling down in the tents of Kedar!"

Now the curtain is drawn back, and we see the interior feelings of the Psalmist. He knows he is in the wrong place in life. Meshech and Kedar are infrequently mentioned in the Bible, but when they appear they are either sons of ancient men or places of uncertain location. Yet, most scholars point to Meshech as being near Colchis on the Black Sea or in ancient Armenia, while Kedar is a spot of uncertain location in the Arabian desert. Exact locations are unimportant; they are chosen to express the extremes of human life and of inhospitable climes. We thus have the distant Meshech, the forbidding Kedar. That is what it feels like when you are constantly under the barrage of deceitful speech; you feel you don't belong in the place you inhabit. You feel you are at the margins of life.

You long to depart from these unhealthy places, but somehow there remains a sort of magnetic appeal to the place where you are. You know if you stay that at least you will keep breathing, while setting out on a journey to another place is fraught with all kinds of uncertainties and dangers. Instead of saying, in 120:5, 'I guess I need to get out of this place,' the Psalmist sinks deeper into his own distress. The word used to express his woe is a *hapax* (once-appearing) *oyyah*, but it is derived from the more frequently appearing (24 times) *oy*, a Jewish term of woe that survives to this day. We all live at times in the Meshechs and Kedars of life, and many and diverse are the causes of this sojourn. Sometimes there appears to be no reasonable way to leave, and we might then liken our sojourn there to life in a pit or a trap. But other times you actually can leave your private Meshechs, your personal Kedars. The Psalmist will show us how this is done in Psalm 121, but now we have to live with the author in his quiet and desperate isolation far from the people of God, so far removed from any sense of order or peace in life. What have been your private Meshechs, your personal Kedars?

6 "For such a long time has my soul lived with those who hate peace!"

Mingled self-pity and desperation continue to pile up as the Psalmist vainly tries to get control of his situation and emotions. The thoughts that burst out in verse 5 now continue to tumble out of his mouth. *Rab* ("abundance" or "much", more than 450 occurrences in the Bible) is the first and most arresting word in the sentence. "Too long" or "too great" is its force. That's what is on his mind, and on our mind, in deepest distress. 'I have put up with this stuff *too long!* I have endured the curses, deception, treachery, false speech, betrayal, *too long!* I have dwelt here *long enough!*' But surprisingly, even when a person concludes that s/he has had it 'up to here,' people keep going back to face the same abuse and deception which caused so much pain. The Psalmist seems to be in this whirlpool of torment, perhaps without a sense of how to escape it. We need to feel the depth of the Psalmist's and our own sense of distance and isolation in order both to endure the rigors of the journey to Jerusalem as well as to endure some of the distress we will find even in the Holy City, distress that is unexpected at first. Still mired, the Psalmist is getting to the point of wanting to depart. But all he can say at this point is "too long!"

7 "I—peace, also when I speak, while these people are for war."

The language of the verse is choppy—perhaps reflecting the emotional turbulence in the author's soul. This verse moves us not an inch further emotionally or geographically. The Psalmist repeats the word from the preceding verse (peace), but characterizes his opponents as "hating" it (v 6), while he, when he speaks, speaks of peace. The final word of the Psalm is "war" (*milchamah*), a fitting word to describe not only the Psalmist's perception of the enemies, but of his own unsettled spirit. He is at war with them and with himself. The Stairway to Heaven or Journey to Jerusalem begins, both literarily and experientially, in an emotional space of distance, isolation and, here, conflict. Rather than expressing the desire to escape in words suggestive of a soaring bird ("Oh that I had wings like a dove, I would fly away and be at rest"—Psalm 55:6), the Psalmist seems to settle in to his grief and isolation, with expressions of self-pity and desire for judgment. What have been the unhealthy places in your life? How long have you stayed there? When did you make your resolve to leave them? Was it difficult to leave them? When we begin to ask these questions we see the value of Psalm 120. Its value rests both in its power in describing our isolation and in our longing for judgment. It is our position as we begin our ascent. In a word, things will go 'up' from here.

Psalm 121 A Song of Ascents

1 I lift up my eyes to the hills—
   from where will my help come?
2 My help comes from the Lord,
   who made heaven and earth.
3 He will not let your foot be moved;
   he who keeps you will not slumber.
4 He who keeps Israel
   will neither slumber nor sleep.
5 The Lord is your keeper;
   the Lord is your shade at your right hand.
6 The sun shall not strike you by day,
   nor the moon by night.
7 The Lord will keep you from all evil;
   he will keep your life.
8 The Lord will keep
   your going out and your coming in
   from this time on and forevermore.

Psalm 121 in a Nutshell

This beloved Psalm has been comforting people ever since it was written. Its stately and confident flow, its simple and transparent images, its repetitive but hopeful direction, all conspire to give us a Psalm both of universal accessibility and enormous depth. Psalm 121 begins the Psalmist's journey from the Meshechs and Kedars of his life to the Holy City of Jerusalem. We aren't told what the primary motivator was to get the Psalmist moving, but moving he is. Often life is that way. Once the pressure of the Meshechs and Kedars of our life has become so intense, we just decide without more ado to leave, to go on pilgrimage, to change the scenery of our lives. Once he starts the journey, he sees a completely different landscape, and this new landscape gives different rhythms to his life. What results from the Psalmist's decision to leave his restricted environment is one of the most beautiful and memorable poems in the Psalter. Sometimes the brave decision to leave the confining Meshechs and Kedars is both the most difficult but most rewarding decision of life.

1 "I shall raise my eyes to the mountains; from where comes my help?"

Writing teachers often tell students that the first rule of effective writing is to vary your sentence structure. The author of this psalm, who often repeats initial words in subsequent verses, seems to have missed that lecture! We are glad that he did. The principal structural item that gives the psalm its confident magnificence is what rhetoricians ancient and modern termed "epanaphora" or, if you want to save money on letters, "anaphora." Derived from a few Greek words meaning "to carry back," it is a literary device defined for the first time in English in a 1678 dictionary as "a figure in which the same word begins several sentences." Anaphora, however, had its first English appearance in George Puttenham's 1589 book *The Arte of English Poesie*, in which he gives the following example:

> "To think on death it is a miserie,
> to think on life it is a vanitie;
> to think on the world verily it is,
> to think that heare man hath no perfit blisse."

(We can see why the movement to standardize spelling started shortly after Puttehnam!). The Psalmist was certainly unaware of how the Greeks and Romans would eventually parse all items of a sentence and conjure up literally hundreds of terms to describe an author's rhetorical armamentarium, but the Psalms are replete with examples of epanaphora. One of the most familiar is in the beginning of Psalm 29, with the anaphora in italics:

> *Ascribe to the Lord*, O heavenly beings,
> *Ascribe to the Lord* glory and strength.
> *Ascribe to the Lord* the glory of his name. . .

There are two other brief points to mention before we begin our exposition. Though we can identify the rhetorical device that "moves" the action of Psalm 121, we ought not to miss the literary effect of it. The Psalmist is now on a Journey to Jerusalem, taking his Stairway to Heaven. Often a journey 'up' is an arduous one. Your foot slips and you have to retrace your last step. You get winded. By repeating the first word of a sentence in the subsequent sentence, the author is, as it were, "retracing" steps that perhaps have slipped on the way to Zion. The Lord won't let you stumble and fall, even though there will be slips along the way as you continue your journey. And, finally, though this is a beloved individual Psalm, we need to see it in its communal dimension. The Lord not only keeps or watches (the verb *shamar,* translated as "preserve/keep/watch/guard," appears six times in this short Psalm) the individual pilgrim but also keeps Israel, the People of God. This is the second of fifteen Psalms in the journey to and residence in Jerusalem. We lived in isolation and deep distress. Now we are climbing to Jerusalem. The glorious journey has begun!

Every long journey begins not only with a single step, as the Chinese tradition has it, but with anticipation and some excitement. The journey brings us out of the old and into the new. He has left the "Meshech" and "Kedar" of his life, and by the time Psalm 121 begins, he is on his way. Maybe it is time for you to leave the worlds that have so long confined you. There is no shame in leaving, especially if the lying lips in the Kedar's and Meshach's of life are eroding your soul. When the Psalmist begins the journey, his eyes are no longer directed to the reality around him, to the lying tongues and deceitful lips; he is now directed to the goal of the journey: Jerusalem/Heaven. Note how the eyes play an important role here and in one other of the Psalms of Ascent. We have a threefold repetition of "eyes" in 123:2, "As the eyes of servants look to (literally "are towards") their master; as the eyes of a maidservant looks to (literally "are towards") her mistress; so our eyes are on (literally "are towards") the Lord our God until he shows us mercy." Here the eyes are to the hills or mountains, a mediate goal to be sure, but these hills will soon give way to more hills and then, finally, to the Holy City.

That Holy City is atop the hills, elsewhere described as "beautiful in situation, the joy of all the earth" (Psalm 48:2). The translation of the second word of 48:2 (*noph*), a one-time appearing word in the Bible, technically called a *hapax legomenon*, is uncertain, and yet the rendering in most translations is "elevation" or "situation." The nearest Hebrew word we know is the familiar *nuph*, which means to wave or move to and fro. The glorious Holy City is the ultimate goal of the journey. Yet the mountains or hills, which the pilgrim see far before seeing Jerusalem, give comfort, direction and longing.

We are to read 121:1 as containing two thoughts—the lifting of eyes and the posing of a question. Many versions, following the Greek translation of the Old Testament, the Septuagint, make it one thought, as if the hills themselves are the source of the help [i.e., "I lift up my eyes to the hills whence comes my help"]. By reading it as two thoughts, with the *meayin* as a true interrogative ("whence?" or "from where?"), we can see the pilgrim trekking, taking a pause, looking upwards at the everlasting hills, and querying further as to the true source of help in life. The words in this verse are remarkably simply and straightforward. Other than the interrogative, all the words appear at least twenty times in the Bible. The way to remember *ezer*, "help/helper," is to associate it with its first two appearances, in Genesis 2. God will make for Adam a "helper" suitable for him (2:18, 20). Now the Psalmist is asking for his true helper. Once you leave the seeming security of even an oppressive condition, you face vulnerability as never before. In addition to the words of beguilement ringing in your ears, you have the uncertainty of the journey. Robbers abound; perhaps dangerous reptiles and noxious plants surround. Are you up for the journey? "Help" or *ezer* is on your mind. What are your sources of help as you climb to Jerusalem, as you mount the Stairway to Heaven?

2 "My help (comes) from the Lord, the maker of the heavens and the earth"

The second appearance of *ezer* ("help/helper") in as many verses leads to two observations. First, if we know Genesis 2:18, 20 and Psalm 121:1, 2, we have mastered four of the 21 appearances of *ezer* in the Bible. Nearly one-fifth of the appearances of this important word are now laid up in our heart, and we haven't even been trying! Sometimes Bible mastery is *so easy*. Not often, but sometimes. The second point is to realize that though the author uses epanaphora/anaphora throughout the Psalm, the technical name of the device where one begins the next sentence with the last word or words of the previous is *anadiplosis* (don't worry, it is good for you, and I won't do this again). The word comes from the Greek and means "to double back upon." Its first appearance in English is again in Puttenham's 1589 classic of rhetorical advice, where he says,

> "As thus: Comforte it is for man to have a wife, Wife chast and wise. The Greeks call this figure *Anadipolsis*, I call him the *Redouble*."

Too bad Puttenham's own appellation for the device didn't stick. When *anadiplosis* occurs, it is usually best to place emphasis on the second appearance. Thus, a good reading of these verses would be: "whence comes my help? MY HELP is from the Lord. . ." When you leave your Meshechs and Kedars, you know you need help. The phrase "the maker of heaven and earth" is so frequent in the Bible as to make us read it almost without thinking, but we should pause for a moment. The nearly identical phrase, with the fifth (!) appearance of *ezer* in the Bible, also appears in a Psalm of Ascent, in 124:8, "Our help (*ezer* is noun) is in the name of the Lord, who made heaven and earth." Psalm 146 expands that description of the maker of heaven and earth by adding one more word ("the sea") and a moral twist to God's creative power: "that made the heavens and the earth, the sea and all that is in it and keeps truth forever," Ps 146:5. An interesting connection between Psalm 146 and 121 is also the appearance of *shamar,* "to keep/ preserve/save," which dominates the action in the second half of Psalm 121 (six occurrences).

We can go further, but not much. When Jonah recites his catechism to sailors wondering what to do to him in Jonah 1:9, he calls God the one who "made the sea and the dry land," though he might have mentioned the latter term just to torment the wave-swelled sailors. Haggai 2:6 uses the fourfold "heavens and earth, sea and dry land" though he varies the word for "dry land" (*charabah*) from Jonah. Indeed, the Genesis story gives us a different word for "make" to describe the creative power of God ("create" or *bara*). Skillful variation of words is the first step in eloquence, in any language, and now we have at least seven words for you to add to your treasury: the Hebrew words for make, create, heavens, earth, sea and two for dry land.

3 "He won't let your foot stumble/be shaken; he (your keeper, that is) won't slumber"

I rendered this literally so that the force of the *epanaphora* is evident. This verse talks about the climb to Jerusalem. In the past few years the rock/mountain-climbing community, as well as the rest of the world, has become fascinated in watching and learning about he exploits of Californian Alex Honnold as he has become the only person to "free solo" (climb without any equipment) the sheer face of El Capitan in Yosemite National Park, California. People who climb worry most about having a firm foothold; thus, having feet free of stumbling is a requirement. The Psalmist's reference to feet is therefore natural, but he chooses the picturesque verb *mot*, "to totter, shake, slip, stumble" to finish the thought.

The Psalms "own" the concept of slipping/faltering/stumbling/tottering/shaking that is captured by the verb *mot*, with nearly two-thirds of its 38 appearances in the Psalms. That makes sense, since people are either shaken (Psalm 13:4) or resolving not to be moved or shaken (Psalm 10:6; 16:8, etc.) throughout the Psalter. But the word "slip" is a better translation here, and the same two words (feet and slip) appear in that richly suggestive and terrifying verse of judgment, Deuteronomy 32:35, "their foot will certainly slip," a verse so suggestive that it became the text for Jonathan Edwards' memorable 1741 Enfield (CT) sermon, "Sinners in the Hands of an Angry God." "Feet" will certainly "slip" in the divine judgment, but in the Journey to Zion the assurance is that your feet will *not* slip.

We might look at the second half of the verse as providing the reason for the confidence of the first part—because the "watcher" will not sleep. Watchers/watchmen are incredibly important for those on a dangerous journey. Instead of your companions just saying to you, "Watch your step!", you can confidently say, "Another is watching *my* steps." Why? Because our watcher doesn't sleep. In fact, the traditional and rarer translation "slumber" is probably better here, because it captures the fact the verb here used, *num* ("to be drowsy/to slumber") is a rare word in Biblical Hebrew—only six appearances. Two of the six are in consecutive verses in this Psalm, and so now you have two words ("helper" and "slumber") whose usages you have a foothold on because of their prevalence in these Psalms or in Genesis 2. Even the sound of it (*noom/num*) makes me drowsy. So we have another way to remember it. Let your biblical mnemonic devices include not just the appearance of the word in a particularly vivid or memorable verse, but an attention to the sound of the word. Focusing on single-syllable Hebrew words like this is a great way to start your vocabulary mastery.

4 "Behold, he doesn't slumber, nor does he sleep—the keeper/watcher of Israel"

Your "personal" watcher of verse 3 is now identified as the "watcher of Israel." Those who embrace a Biblical faith have always affirmed what the Psalmist does here, that their God is the God of Israel. The thought here adds little to the preceding verse, but serves as an intensification of it. And the intensification also functions to slow us down as readers. We all have access to internet-based programs that help us read faster, but a good deal of wisdom comes from slowing down as we read. Slowing down, focusing on and savoring language helps us refine our understanding. The little word variation here (by combining "sleep" with "slumber") invites us to a brief consideration of Hebrew words for sleeping. Here we have the combination "slumber" and "sleep" (*num* and *yashen*). *Num* ("slumber") appears with the noun form of *shenah* or *yashen* ("sleep", 24 appearances) in Psalm 76:5, the "stout of heart. . .slumber in their sleep/fall asleep". One can "lie down and slumber" (*num* and *shakab*) in Isaiah 56:10, but normally, if two verbs are used, it is *shakab and yashen* ("lie down and sleep"). The most memorable combination of these *shakab* and *yashen* is in Psalm 4:8, "In peace I will both lie down and sleep." The combination used in 121:4, *num* and *yashen,* is unique in the Bible.

Yet we can do a bit more with sleep. When Jonah went down below deck to catch some shut-eye when the boat threatened to break up, he "lay down and fell into a deep sleep." The verb used here for falling into a "deep sleep" is *radam* (1:5), the noun form of which, *tardemah,* is also the anesthetic-like deep sleep brought upon Adam by God before creating Eve (Genesis 2:21). Then, finally, in an obscure passage, with the rare delight of back to back *hapaxes*, we have a negative description of false watchmen (different word than in Ps 121) who are "mute dogs" that don't bark, "sleepers/dreamers, lying down, loving to slumber" (Isaiah 56:10). We thus have another seven words, this time for "lying down" (*shakab*) and "slumbering" (*num*) and "sleeping" (*yashen*) and "dreaming" (*chalom*) and "sleep" (*shenah*) and "deep sleep" (noun, *tardemah*) and "deep sleep" (verb, *radam*). As we climb to Jerusalem on our stairway to heaven, with each step we add a word, until we know the language and very rhythms of biblical faith. While you are in class or just before you fall asleep at night, recite these words. This exercise may improve your life.

5 "The Lord is your keeper, the Lord is your protection/shade at your right hand"

We can play a Psalm 121 game. The game is to try to figure out how many people are likely speaking in this Psalm. There are almost as many different theories as there are interpreters. Some see verse 1 as Person One speaking, with verse 2 as a response to the question of verse 1 by Person Two. Then some see verse 3 as a continuation of Person Two's speaking, though others see Person Three entering, to add to the mix. Or, some see one speaker behind all the verses. In my mind it really doesn't really matter, though the thought of one or two other people singing in antiphonal response to the initial inquirer adds luster to an already lustrous poem. In verse 5 we have the third appearance of "keeper" or "watcher" (vv 3, 4, 5; derived from the common verb *shamar* in all three instances) so far. The repetitive intonation of the word adds deeply to the sense of security felt by one on pilgrimage. We need constantly to repeat such a thought, since we have no other refuge if the Keeper is absent.

Just as I read Jeremiah 9 as providing the meaning-giving context to the distressful cry of Psalm 120, so I see Psalm 91 as another text that gives depth to the brief affirmations of these verses. In Psalm 121 we have God as a protection on the right side, so that sun doesn't strike by day nor the moon by night. But in Psalm 91 we have a richly-layered exploration of the threats to the believer as well as the protections provided by God to handle those threats. Thus, in order to deepen our appreciation of Psalm 121, let's pause and review a few verses from Psalm 91.

The link between the two Psalms is the simple word *tsel*, translated "shade" or "shadow." The Lord is your "shade" is the affirmation of Ps 121:5; those who dwell in the "shade" or "shadow" of the Almighty are the subject of the first several verses of Psalm 91. Let's consider 91:1-2,

91:1 "The dwellers in the secret place of the Most High, they shall dwell in the shade of the Almighty"

God has many names in the Scripture, perhaps as many as the Muslims attribute to Allah in their sacred book. Here we have "the Most High," whose first two appearances, interestingly enough, are in the mouths of non-Israelites. Melchizedek the high priest was the first to use the word as a name for God (Genesis 14:20) and Balaam followed with that designation (Numbers 24:16). Shaddai, the Almighty (91:1), however, is first used by God in a dialogue with Abram just as he is undergoing his name-change operation (Genesis 17:1). In Psalm 91 we are talking about living or settling into the protection of that God and not just, as in Psalm 121, looking at it as an accompaniment of the journey. In Psalm 91:1, *tsel* is used synonymously with *sether*, "hiding place" and that latter noun is derived from the verb of nearly the same spelling, meaning to conceal or hide. This is not the place for a full exposition of Ps 91, but suffice it to say that the word describing this "hiding place" or place of "secrecy," has a range of meanings in Scripture that take us all the way from a description of a place of divine protection to a hiding place, to what is frequently done in secret (such as backbiting or tale-bearing). One other feature of Psalm 91:1 is the presence of verbs as the first and last words. "Dwell" and "lodge/abide" sandwich the thoughts, as if the affirmation of presence and abiding is the thing which incorporates or includes everything in between.

91:2 "I will say to the Lord, 'My refuge and my fortress.' My God, I trust in Him"

Psalm 121 is so preoccupied with moving quickly on the journey that the vocabulary of journey and protection is limited, but in Psalm 91 we can go deeper into the contours of the divine protection or sheltering assumed by the one climbing to Zion. Terminology dripping with theological and visual power emerges in Psalm 91. First, we have two more terms or names for God: "Yahweh" and "My God." If a three-fold cord cannot quickly be broken, what about *four* divine names in two verses? But we have more than the names of God to give protection. The term translated "refuge" (*machaseh*) in 91:1, though appearing 20 times in the Bible, is really "owned" by the Psalms, most memorably in one of Martin Luther's favorite Psalms, "God is our refuge and strength" (46:1). It is frequently paired in the Psalms with *oz*, "strength" or "might." Here, however, it is linked with *metsudah*, which originally suggested a kind of fort or castle for protection against human foes (I Samuel 22:4, 5) but then was transferred to a divine attribute. Surprisingly it can also carry the notion of a net, though I suppose that calling God one's "net" might not resonate much with anyone. One would think that the common verb *batach* ("to trust," 120 appearances) would have been frequently used from the very beginning of the Bible, but it is almost completely absent from the Pentateuch and doesn't really get warmed up until it is used about 10 times in II Kings 18-19 to describe King Hezekiah's attitude toward God. (I think the verb *aman*, "to believe," a slightly less-frequently-appearing word than *batach*, functions as the Pentateuchal substitute for *batach*, and it appears more than a dozen times in Genesis and Exodus alone).

Back to Psalm 121.

6-8 "By day the sun will not strike, neither the moon by night. The Lord will keep you from all sorts of evil; He will preserve your life. The Lord will keep your goings and comings until eternity"

While commentators have tied themselves into knots trying to describe exactly the kind of danger the moon might bring to travelers by night, I think it is better to understand the mention of celestial bodies as referring to generic threats that stalk the traveler. Thus, one has the assurance of complete protection provided by the Lord to the traveler to Zion. Does the repeated use of "keep" or "preserve" and the relative simplicity of the language (preserve only from "evil") in Psalm 121 undermine or detract from its literary power? Not at all, when considering the context of its appearance. The pilgrim is on a journey. When facing a journey, you need almost total focus on your journey, with only the assurance that the journey itself is protected. Thus the simple language, rather than detracting from the Psalm, adds to its potent majesty. We are on the journey; we need protection from evil, from all kinds of evils, 24/7, and we need to be saved/preserved/kept (which capture the broad sweep of *shamar*). But that is not all we need.

Journeys are such complex things. One needs equipment, food, means of protection from possible enemies, both human and reptilian, a means of keeping harmony among people, sturdy clothing, good health. In such a situation one doesn't think so much about words but about the climb. But Psalm 91, which functions as our great "commentary" on Psalm 121, allows us to go deeper into the emotions of a traveler, emotions that had no room for expression in Psalm 121. If the author of Psalm 121 could appear on a modern talk show, he would say, "Yes, Psalm 91 perfectly described the emotions I felt during my journey." As we saw, Psalm 91 began with names and attributes of the "God of four names," but it continues with specific details of the kind of protection that this God provides.

The description in 91:3-16 is so rich and suggestive that I will only give it in English here, with a few comments on select Hebrew words in the text that form a more direct bridge to Psalm 121, lest we get borne into another world. As you read Psalm 91 again and again, you begin to see it as a commentary on *both* Psalms 120 and 121. A few of those linguistic dependences will be noted below; a full exposition awaits another time.

If you aren't interested in a detailed comparison of Psalms, you may skip to the "Notes" at the end of this chapter or to Psalm 122.

91:3 For he will deliver you from the snare of the fowler
    and from the deadly pestilence;
4 he will cover you with his pinions,
    and under his wings you will find refuge;
    his faithfulness is a shield and buckler.
5 You will not fear the terror of the night,
    or the arrow that flies by day,
6 or the pestilence that stalks in darkness,
    or the destruction that wastes at noonday.
7 A thousand may fall at your side,
    ten thousand at your right hand,
    but it will not come near you.
8 You will only look with your eyes
    and see the punishment of the wicked.
9 Because you have made the Lord your refuge,
    the Most High your dwelling place,
10 no evil shall befall you,
    no scourge come near your tent.
11 For he will command his angels concerning you
    to guard you in all your ways.
12 On their hands they will bear you up,
    so that you will not dash your foot against a stone.
13 You will tread on the lion and the adder,
    the young lion and the serpent you will trample
    under foot.
14 Those who love me, I will deliver;
    I will protect those who know my name.
15 When they call to me, I will answer them,
    I will be with them in trouble,
    I will rescue them and honor them.

> 16 With long life I will satisfy them,
>   and show them my salvation.

91:3, The deliverance. Though the language of Psalm 121 is all about "keeping" or "preserving" (the verb *shamar* is used six times), Psalm 120 is about deliverance (*natsal*, v 2). Psalm 120 uses that verb to talk about "deliverance" from lying and deceptive lips, but Psalm 121 talks about "preserving" in the midst of traveling dangers. Psalm 91 affirms *both* concepts, using both *shamar* and *natsar*. It both talks about "deliverance" from traveling dangers/the dangers "out there" on the road (*natsal*, v 3), as well as the preservation (*shamar*, v 11) with which God covers the faithful. In addition, two appearances of the word refuge (*machaseh*) in Psalm 91 (vv 2, 9) emphasize the protective and preservative care of God.

91:5-6. The times of the day. Whereas Psalm 121 only talked about preservation from the sun in the day and the moon at night, in Psalm 91 we have a much more detailed catalogue of potential dangers, keyed to a more detailed "clock" than in Psalm 121. Here we will not fear the terror (*pachad* is the word) of the night nor the arrow (*chets* is the word) that wings by day (v 5). "Terror" is a richly textured word in the Scripture, and its usages go all the way from a name of God connected with Isaac (Genesis 31:42) to the abject terror felt by the Egyptian troops vainly trying to escape the rushing waters of the sea (Exodus 15:16). Terror stalks many of our paths, though we are often slow to realize this. We saw the "arrows" in Psalm 120, the punishment which the Psalmist wishes on his enemies (120:4). But Psalm 91 gives us double for our money by adding verse 6, breaking the day into twice as many segments as Psalm 121. In addition to trials in day and night, Psalm 91 talks about how one will be delivered from the plague (*deber*) in the darkness (*ophel*) and the destruction (*qeteb*) that violently destroys (*shud*) in noontime (*tsohar*). A fruitful harvest of words is here, no doubt, but what is most evident is the doubling of the references to time in Psalm 91.

Interestingly enough, the word for "plague" or "pestilence" has the identical root characters as the common Hebrew word for "word" or "deed." A plague, then, is the "deed par excellence," the "deed" that ravishes. Biblical Hebrew has a number of words to describe darkness, and the one in Psalm 91:6 (pronounced *ophel*) only appears nine times in the Bible, two-thirds of which are in Job. In Job this is the fearsome, utter gloom that Job wanted to cover the day of his birth (Job 3:6), a darkness so profound that nothing can be seen. Yet, by using the word here (91:6), the Psalmist, as it were "redeems Job," or says as if, in words of another Psalm, "the darkness is not dark to thee, but the darkness shines as the day" (Ps 139:12, using a different word for "darkness"). God also delivers from this kind of horrifying darkness. *Qeteb,* translated "destruction," is a rare word in Biblical Hebrew, appearing only three times and always in poetic contexts. The verbal root doesn't exist, though the large Hebrew dictionary (the BDB) says that this "unused root" means "to cut off" or "to ruin." If it doesn't exist, how do they know what it means? I suppose, though, this isn't a wild guess. Again, the word for "wasting" is unique: this is its only appearance in the Bible. Yet, we can see lurking behind the word for "wasting," *shud,* the relatively more common word (57 appearances) *shadad,* "to destroy" or "to devastate." One of its prominent usages in the Scripture is in that most vengeful Psalm, where the Babylonians are called "the one to be destroyed" (*hashshedudah,* 137:8). Poets have license to change words seemingly at will, though the transformation of *shadad* into *shud* is getting perilously close to *shaddai,* one of the names of God in Psalm 91.

91:10. Lest we feel that the text of Psalm 91 is drawing us away from that of Psalms 120 and 121 because of the detailed descriptions of distress in Psalm 91, we return to a shared word in 91:10, *raah,* "evil" and a shared, though not explicitly mentioned in Psalm 121, concept. The evil from which the Lord "preserves" us in 121:7 is the evil that is not permitted to "befall" us in 91:10.

We are in the same linguistic and idea world. 91:10 uses the few-times-appearing verb *anah*, "to befall" or "happen", to describe the evil that won't come our way. Other verbs such as *pagash, qara, qadam,* all appear more frequently than *anah* and all carry the connotation of meeting or encountering or befalling. In fact, the five other appearances of *anah* don't really provide a clearly-defined lexical world. It appears once in a legal text (Exodus 21:13) to describe someone "falling into" another's hands, and then it occurs twice in Numbers 14:11 in an expression: *ad-anah*, which in context has to mean "how long"? Then, in one other place it clearly means "to quarrel" (II Kings 5:7). Only in Proverbs 12:21 does it seem to share, unequivocally, the meaning of our text, and indeed the idea world there completely overlaps that of 91:10. Proverbs 12:21 has, "no trouble/sorrow/evil befalls the righteous." We see a different word for "evil" here, and we rejoice that we can build our vocabulary, but then the rest of the verse says, "but the wicked are full of evil," (with *ra* for "evil"), and we are back in our familiar world. The idea explicitly mentioned in Psalm 91:10 that seems absent at first from Psalm 121 is reference to one's tent. No evil comes near one's tent. Surely as travelers were on their Highway to Heaven in Psalm 121, one of the major concerns was the nighttime security of the tents. Psalm 91 "anticipates" that anxiety by providing that the Lord won't permit evil to come near one's tent. Perfect overlap.

91:14. The NRSV has "I will protect those who know my name." But now that we see Psalm 91 as a commentary on the plans and movements of Psalm 120-121, we can read those words more precisely. The Hebrew has, literally, "I will make him/her inaccessibly high because s/he knows my name." With the potential confusion of those words, no wonder the NRSV retreated to the safe confines of "protect," when translating the verse, but that's not what it really says. *sagab* occurs 20 times in the Bible, and either describes the "exalted" God (Job 36:22) or the way that a person is lifted/exalted to safety by God (Job 5:11). The verb appears seven times in the Psalms, and in each case it emphasizes a secure high place where the Lord leads the believer (see, for example, Ps 20:1 or 69:29). Once we realize the "120-121" context of Psalm 91, we see that this promise of lifting inaccessibly high is wonderfully connected to the movement of Psalm 121. They are on the way to Zion. No time, really, for fancy words and detailed exploration of the dangers that threaten and the ways that God delivers. God is just the one who "preserves" or "keeps." Yet Psalm 91 rescues the Psalmist literarily by providing language of comfort and specificity, specifically that is tied to four times of the day and is targeted to relieve anxiety and lend encouragement.

91:15. The Psalm concludes with a plethora of familiar Psalm 120-121-type of words. We have the identical words for call and answer in 91:15 as in Psalm 120:1. In Psalm 120:1 the verbs are in the past tense; in 91:15 they are in the future. Both past and future are "covered" by the God who leads the pilgrim to inaccessibly high places. Lest we missed the point, Psalm 91:15 also talks about "deliverance" (literally "I will deliver him/her") and "in (time) of trouble," words shared with Psalm 120:1, 2. It is almost as if the text of Psalm 91 is *screaming* for us to take note of its filling up the meaning of 120-121. But Psalm 91 gives us a bonus word, a word that rewards those who diligently keep reading. Not only will God be with the pilgrim traveler in his/her distresses and deliver them, but God will "honor" him/her (verb is the common *kabad*). The full scope of that "honor" isn't exposited in Psalm 91, other than to say that God will satisfy the believer (91:16), but if we look at the Psalter as antiphonal call and response, we might see Psalms 122-134, the rest of the Psalms of Ascent, as filling out the contours of the "honor" that Psalm 91:16 only hints at. That is, just as Psalm 91 "specializes" in identifying the perils and specifying the deliverance along the journey, yet is somewhat silent on the results after this deliverance comes, so

Psalms 120-134 are rather sparing in language about the journey to Jerusalem yet are quite full in their description of the life "in the inaccessibly high place" after one has arrived in Jerusalem. Psalm not only calls to Psalm, but each provides what each other lacks to lend a symphonic richness to the spiritual life.

Notes

_____

_____

_____

_____

_____

_____

_____

_____

_____

_____

_____

_____

_____

_____

_____

_____

_____

_____

_____

_____

_____

Psalm 122 A Song of Ascents. Of David.

1 I was glad when they said to me,
    "Let us go to the house of the Lord!"
2 Our feet are standing
    within your gates, O Jerusalem.
3 Jerusalem—built as a city
    that is bound firmly together.
4 To it the tribes go up,
    the tribes of the Lord,
    as was decreed for Israel,
    to give thanks to the name of the Lord.
5 For there the thrones for judgment were set up,
    the thrones of the house of David.
6 Pray for the peace of Jerusalem:
    "May they prosper who love you.
7 Peace be within your walls,
    and security within your towers."
8 For the sake of my relatives and friends
    I will say, "Peace be within you."
9 For the sake of the house of the Lord our God,
    I will seek your good.

Psalm 122 in a Nutshell

In this Psalm we arrive in Jerusalem. That was quick! And we will *still* have a dozen Psalms to go in our Psalms of Ascent. The journey is finished but, from another perspective, it is just beginning. In this Psalm we arrive in the confines of Jerusalem, the goal of our journey, but once we are there, once in the inaccessibly high place of salvation, having climbed the Stairway to Heaven amid all the threats and dangers, we realize that the original goal of our journey (to get to Jerusalem/Heaven/salvation) was only the first leg of the trip. It is like a student who puts all of his or her effort into study to secure a BA but then hears the commencement speaker tell him or her that life is just starting (hence the word "commencement"). The degree should open doors to the future, but that is all it does. It provides a place to begin. So, our arrival in Jerusalem will, figuratively, be greeted with, "Welcome...now, there is *so much* to see and do!" Life often begins *after* you think you have reached the goal of your longings and the target of your strivings.

1 "I rejoiced in their saying to me, 'The House of Yahweh, let's go there'"

The fact of the pilgrims' having arrived in Jerusalem, the goal of the journey, isn't even mentioned. There are no shared references or banter regarding the arduousness of the journey or the feelings of elation as the glistening lights or looming buildings of the Holy City came into view. There is no reference to whether Days Inn was full or how one found one's lodging on the first night. There is no discussion of bunions and cuts and scrapes or of the sighs of relief that no doubt were uttered by many on arrival. We are in the city, ready for the next stage of life. And the first word is joy. The Hebrew verb for "rejoice" or "be glad" is *samach*, a wonderfully explosive word.

Because of its prevalence in the Bible (150 appearances), we might call it 'joy's generic brand,' though it is not the less sincere for being so prevalent. Though it appears once in Leviticus, it really doesn't get 'warmed up' in its appearances until Deuteronomy but then, in nine memorable passages, it bursts on the scene with clarity and fervor. Its first Deuteronomic appearance is, interestingly enough also connected with the Holy City or, in Deuteronomy's language, "the place that the Lord will choose out of all your tribes as his habitation to put his name there" (12:5). When there, you shall "rejoice" (*samach* is verb) in all you put your hand to. . ." (12:7). Lest we miss the message, five verses later the Israelites are exhorted to "rejoice before the Lord" (*samach* again is the verb, 12:12). The related noun *simchah* appears nearly 100 times, memorably in Psalm 4:7, "You have given gladness (*simchah*) to my heart, more than when their grain and wine abound." More specialized uses of verbs for "rejoice" also appear in Scripture, as in the famous passage, "Rejoice, greatly, O daughter of Zion" (Zecharaiah 9:9, using *gil*, which appears a 'mere' 45 times). The laborious climb is over; rejoicing fills our hearts. The recently-arrived pilgrim goes to the house of God, right to the center of faith. Arrive in the city, and don't stay in the outskirts. Go right to the heart of your faith, to the heart of God. That is the goal of the pilgrimage; that is why one climbs the hills.

2 "Standing firm are our feet in front of your gates, O Jerusalem"

The crescendo of joy grows as words of security and solidity replace those that focused on dealings with lying neighbors (Psalm 120) or the labor of the journey (Psalm 91 interpreting Psalm 121). Now the Psalmist is "standing." Even more, the Psalmist's "feet" are standing. One might at first see this as a kind of small point (i.e., what other body part would be standing?), until you realize that this is a direct "response" to Psalm 121:3, "He will not allow your foot to stumble/slip." Now one's "feet" (same word, *regel*, though in the plural here—"our feet") are "standing" (*amad*) rather than in danger of "slipping" (*mot*—121:3). We have security squared, with both rejoicing and standing. And, to add to the intensity and intimacy of the moment, Jerusalem and its gates are addressed as if alive. It is as if one has reached the end of a long journey and says to one's home or destination, "Hi walls, we've made it!" Already a level of intimacy is intimated, which will grow until we see the wonderfully fetching image of intimate communal unity in Psalm 133.

3, 4 "Jerusalem is built as a united and compact city, joined all together. The tribes go up there, the tribes of the Lord, as a testimony of Israel's giving thanks to the name of the Lord"

As long as you realize that these two verses weren't written for English-language speakers, you are fine. All commentators point to the relative opacity of the first part (v 3), while the second part (v 4) uses a play on words that can't be captured easily in English. Before we try our best to suss out some meaning, let's pause and get our bearings. The author is now in Jerusalem, the goal of the trek, and is heading straight for the house of God. Then, before getting there, the author "pauses" for the rest of the Psalm, to take in the scope and meaning of this great place. Don't try to get to the heart or the center of things too quickly; rather, look around and take in the grandeur, the history, the meaning of the sacred city before heading to the holy precincts. Sacred things become even more so for you if you study the context in which they are presented. That is what our author does.

He begins with a description of the city, using an image that isn't crystalline. The two words controlling the image are derived from the verb *chabar,* which can literally be rendered "to join" or "to ally" or "to unite," and the adverb *yachad,* a common word meaning "together." The verb *chabar* appears 28 times in the Bible, a full half of which appear in a few chapter in Exodus describing how the curtains of the Tabernacle are "joined" to each other (e.g., Exodus 26:3, 6, 9, 11). Most scholars see Psalm 122:3 describing either the "compactness" of Jerusalem or, if a period after the exile is contemplated, the "reconstructing" of the temple. I would tend to look at this from the perspective of the other word used: *yachad* ("together"). *Yachad* not only appears here but is the central word driving the second to last Psalm of Ascent (133). Thus, when we read this Psalm in the context of the entire Psalms of Ascent, meaning emerges.

"Togetherness" rather than rebuilding or compactness, is in view. Even though the author may have had *some* companions on his Psalm 121 journey, upon arrival in the sacred confines he is surrounded by people from *all* the tribes. There are the Naphtalites, there the Danites! Such a feeling of "togetherness" in this "united" or "together" city! Why not, then, see the author hinting at the concept of unity that will find its fruition in the joy felt by the community at the unity experienced in Psalm 133, a unity instantiated and visually presented by oil running down the high priest's beard? Jerusalem is "tight together" or "united," and its "togetherness" is central to the author's journey.

Verse 4 continues this idea by emphasizing a thought that is now familiar to us—Jerusalem as goal of the tribes' journey. But the "action" of verse four is in an alliteration, *eduth* (testimony or law) combined with the verb *yadah. Yadah* has several meanings, among them to "throw" or "to give thanks." We can try to make sense of the verb by saying that it was a law or requirement to give thanks to God, but that is 'legalizing' two words when really the emphasis is simply on the sounds. Repeat the actual Hebrew words of 122:4, *eduth (leyisrael) lehodoth,* a few times and you are lifted up and carried away to a realm of praise. Recall Jonah 1:5, where Jonah's sea-tossed ship was in danger of shattering. Literally, the words in that verse mean "was reckoned to be about to shatter," but when you realize that the point is the alliteration, *hishbar lehishaber,* you just calm down and let the sounds minister to you. So, say it five times, *eduth (leyisrael) lehodoth,* and you have the joyful sounds echoing in your ears. When they are just translated "testimony" and "give thanks" in English, it may ring "true," but it doesn't really "ring." Our concept of clarity is challenged and expanded when we have resonant-sounding words, words that sometimes don't yield the clearest "meaning," that are the focal point of our verse. They encourage us to get lost in their sounds.

5 "Because the thrones for judgment sit there, thrones for the house of David"

Before we get too carried away in the spiritual "high" of the moment, standing directly before the temple and enjoying the "unity" of the city and the "praise" due the place, the author brings us down to earth by stressing that Jerusalem is also the civil capital of the people. A civil capital is not only a place of commerce and legislation but, above all, a place where disputes are settled and law is made clear. "Thrones of judgment" points to the judicial function of Jerusalem in the life of the people of God. Lest we miss the point we need only to recall that when Solomon was first appointed King over Israel and prayed his great prayer in I Kings 3, the thing he asked for was not deeper spiritual insight or a "closer walk with Thee," but rather for wisdom, wisdom to discern how to govern a people (I Kings 3:9). One might marvel at the walls and fortresses of the city; one might be spiritually awe-struck at the temple and its appointments, but one ought never to forget the dual mention of thrones here, thrones that stand for judgment, justice, and wise governance of the people of God.

6-7 "Pray for Jerusalem's peace; may those that love you be at ease. May there be peace in your gates and quietness in your palaces"

The first three Hebrew words of verse 6 make for an alliterative feast, a feast that isn't even a snack if all we knew was English: *shalu shelom yerushalam.* The "sh's" keep washing over us, telling our souls to "hush, hush, hush" as the peace which the author prays for comes upon the city. The author "purchases" this alliteration at the cost of using a verb normally translated "ask" or "request" (*shaal*) as "pray" here. Sometimes meaning has to be s-t-r-e-t-c-h-e-d in order to get the sound ringing powerfully in our ears. Recall that at the end of the first Psalm of Ascent the author talked about his companions being for war while he longed for peace (120:7). Peace, then, was on the author's brain. And now he wishes this peace on the Holy City. In fact, we can extend our alliteration to a fourth word; "be at ease" renders *yishlayu.* (The verb is the rare *shale,* appearing only three other places, most notably in Job 3:26, where Job complains that he is *not* at ease). Then, with the final word, "those who love you," we return to the "normalcy" of language. So, here is how the verse is pronounced: *shalu shelom yerushalam yishlayu ohabayik.* As with my earlier point about the alliteration of 122:4, the power is not always in the literal meaning of the words but in their sounds. Here, as the hush of night settles on the Holy City, the author wishes that same kind of comforting peace for the city.

In order to get to this alliteration, however, the author has to 'sacrifice' meaning—that is, as mentioned, he chooses a generic word for "ask" rather than the expected word(s) for "pray" as his first word; the fourth word, translated "be at ease," is sometimes rendered "prosper," but it really shares more with the concept of tranquility than prosperity. Thus asking for ease for those that love Jerusalem, a literal reading, might not be as "accurate" as choosing the "proper" words for "praying" and "prospering," which Biblical Hebrew has in abundance. But literal meaning is sacrificed to resonant sonority—maybe we should learn some lessons from that.

The implication, thus, is that meaning may be more in the sounds than in the words. Verse 7 reinforces the meaning of verse 6. But the alliteration continues in verse 7, where *shalom* and *shalvah* are paired ("peace" and "ease"), though now connected with walls and palaces. The "walls and palaces" also appear together in another 'admire Jerusalem'-type of Psalm, Psalm 48 which may be read as a commentary or midrash on this verse of Psalm 122. Listen to Psalm 48:12-13,

> "Walk about Zion, go all around it, count its towers, consider well its ramparts ("walls"); go through its citadels ("palaces").

The verbs of Psalm 48:13 are much more sophisticated and rare than the simple "let there be peace" of Psalm 122:7. In Psalm 48 one is to "lay in heart/place in (your) heart" (*shith* is the verb) the walls and "consider" (*pasag*, a *hapax* that no one is quite sure how to translate) her "citadels" or "palaces" (*armon*, the same word as in 122:7). Some translations render *pasag* as "visit" or "tour" or "go through." Just as the author of Psalm 121 was more concerned to emphasize the divine protection against threatened harms than to enumerate those harms (Psalm 91 does that), so the author of Psalm 122 is more interested in wishing an alliterative blessing on pilgrim and city alike than on worrying about how to look at the walls and palaces/citadels. The *shalvah*, "ease" or "tranquility," of 122:7 is closely related in word form and meaning to the *shalah* in verse 6. It reinforces the "peace" theme of the last four verses of the psalm.

8-9 "For the sake of my brothers and companions alike, I will most sincerely ask for your peace. For the sake of the house of the Lord our God, I will see your good"

We conclude with two parallel phrases beginning with *lemaan,* "for the sake of," in verses 8-9. The purpose of the prayer begun in verse 6 is that there be peace for companion and brethren; that there be "good" for Jerusalem. We return here to simple words, with no alliteration, but we also have the repeated theme of peace and, for the first time, "good" (*tob*), which no doubt occupies the same meaning universe as "peace" and "ease" and "tranquility." Even the verbs are commonplace—and they work better alliteratively in English than in Hebrew, for once! One "speaks" for peace, with an appropriate deferential word (*na);* one "seeks" (verb is *baqash;* more than 200 appearances in the Bible) the "good" of Jerusalem. The goal of the journey, seemingly, is attained. The traveler is now in Jerusalem, describing the city, wishing peace for it and for his companions, luxuriating in the unity of the city, giving thanks, and seemingly reveling in the new life atop the Stairway to Heaven. But we are only one-fifth of the way on our journey on the Psalms of Ascents, which suggests that most of life now takes place in the complexities of life in the City of God. We can hardly wait to see what these complexities (and joys) are.

Psalm 122 A Song of Ascents. Of David.

Notes

_____

_____

_____

_____

_____

_____

_____

_____

_____

_____

_____

_____

_____

_____

_____

_____

_____

_____

_____

_____

_____

_____

Psalm 123 A Song of Ascents

1 To you I lift up my eyes,
   O you who are enthroned in the heavens!
2 As the eyes of servants
   look to the hand of their master,
as the eyes of a maid
   to the hand of her mistress,
so our eyes look to the Lord our God,
   until he has mercy upon us.
3 Have mercy upon us, O Lord, have mercy upon us,
   for we have had more than enough of contempt.
4 Our soul has had more than its fill
   of the scorn of those who are at ease,
   of the contempt of the proud.

Psalm 123 in a Nutshell

Surprisingly, or perhaps not so surprisingly after all, once one has arrived in the Holy City to get one's bearings, has expressed good wishes to all and has prayed for the ease and peace of Jerusalem, problems emerge. Problems arise, even in Jerusalem. Prosperity and peace can be ephemeral phenomena, and they are often driven out either by the stabbing reminders of the past, worry about the future or a renewed focus on conflict right before our eyes. In any case, the attitude of the Psalmist changes fairly dramatically here. In Psalm 121 he was the expectant traveler; in Psalm 122 he experienced the triumphant arrival. Now, he is the needy suppliant. As you read this song, try to follow the language of dependence and distress, of request and regret. We will begin to see that once the preliminary goal has been reached (arrival in the Holy City), complexities develop.

1-2a "To you I lift up my eyes, you who sit in the heavens. Behold, as the eyes of servants to the hand of their master, as the eyes of a maid to the hand of her mistress, so our eyes are toward the Lord our God"

The Psalmist first lifted up eyes to the hills (same verb *nasa*) in Psalm 121:1. It is good for him to get into the habit of raising his eyes, for now in the Holy City he lifts them still higher, to the one who is in the heavens. The word "eyes" appears four times in the first two verses; we might say that in these verses the "eyes" have it! Though the eyes appear four times, it really is two sets of two "eyes" that come into view. "My" or "our" eyes encircle references to "servants'" eyes. The Psalmist likens himself to such a servant, who waits in quiet expectation for grace from the master. Despite the apparent peacefulness and order of these words, tension will arise in the Psalm as it unfolds.

Though the inclination and desire is to lift up the eyes higher and higher, above the mountains and even to the heavens, the sobering realities of earth will soon bring our author back to earth. We are, after all, tethered to earth, and we both need to and long to return to it. Now, however, we just have the lifting up of eyes, and we are instructed. That is the place to go, the place to begin our day in the city of God. Once we have counted all the stones in the pavement of the Heavenly City, we turn our eyes to God. God is called the one who "sits in the heavens." Other designations are possible, of course, such as one who is "enthroned between the cherubim" (Isaiah 37:16) or "sitting enthroned on the cherubim" (Psalm 99:1), but this one works well. We wait with patient expectation, like the servant waits for direction or approbation from the master.

2 "until he is gracious to us"

The amount of repetition in such a short Psalm is stunning. Apart from the title, it is 39 Hebrew words in length, but in those words are four appearances of "eyes," three of "have mercy," two of "contempt", two of "filled with" and two of "greatly," which modifies the "filled with." Thus a full one-third of Psalm consists of 'repeats.' The first rule of becoming a good writer I learned in my youth was to vary my sentence structure, and the second rule I learned was to vary my vocabulary, even in describing the same thing. The Psalms seem to violate both of those 'rules' with regularity. The Psalms are not unique in this. Rhythmic repetition is a staple in many of the 305 sacred songs of ancient China, the 诗经 (shi1jing1), probably written about the same time as the Psalms of Israel. Upon further reflection, this makes sense. These are songs; songs derive their power from the familiar chorus as well as the new verses.

Our eyes look to God until God have mercy on us or is gracious to us. The concept of mercy, graciousness, or favor, so prevalent in the Scripture, appears here and 77 other places through the verb *chanan*. Though liberally sprinkled throughout the Hebrew Bible, it is especially beloved in the Psalms, with more than thirty appearances there. One noteworthy example is in Psalm 67:1, where it is linked with "blessing," another significant biblical word:"(May) God show favor to us, bless us, make his face shine upon us" (the first two verbs are *chanan* and *barak*). You would have thought that with feet inside the Holy City, with the experience of salvation behind them, with eyes to God, the new arrival would have had more than enough spiritual ammunition to ward off any foe. But almost as soon as the pilgrim settles into Jerusalem, he is asking for a triple supply of grace (*chanan* appears three times in two verses). Why? Let's get to that.

3"Be gracious to us, O Lord, be gracious to us, for we have had our fill of contempt."

Now we see the reason for a three-fold request for mercy. "We've had it up to *here* with contempt!" Though the Psalmist does not link these words explicitly with the cloying and enervating feeling of being attacked by lying lips and deceptive tongues in Psalm 120, he does bring us into a nearby linguistic neighborhood, the neighborhood of contempt and scorn. If deception lives in the world of causing one to believe what is false, to delude, to hoodwink, to take someone in, contempt occupies the space of treating of little account, or as vile or worthless. Yet, the result is the same: a person deceived or treated as worthless feels humiliated, abased, lowered. That is, the Psalmist wants so much to *climb up* to the heights of the Holy City and, indeed, he has "arrived" there, but the experiences of life that still cling to his heart want to *bring him down* to the depths. Thus, his imagined reality is in the heights but, as this Psalm unfolds, his felt reality is in the depths. And, these are depths that are not simply wished or prayed away.

The Psalmist will return to them with brief, but hard-hitting eloquence in Psalm 130, near the end of the Psalms of Ascent. Life in the depths while residing in the heights is often a dual reality for those who embrace the life of faith. The final phrase, "had our fill of" contempt is literally "sated more than enough." The word for "sated" is *saba*, whose first 11 (out of 99) appearances in the Bible are connected with "eating one's fill" (e.g., Ex 16:8, 12) but it begins to take on a metaphorical meaning in the towering literary imagination of Job. There the author talks about God's "filling me with bitterness" (9:18) or about how his days are "full of turmoil" (14:1). Lamentations, taking up where Job left off, also talks about how God has filled him with bitterness (3:15) and then wishes that his enemies would be "filled with reproach/shame" (*cherpah* is the word for "reproach/shame, 3:30). The Psalmist tries to 'rescue' the idea of fullness by talking about a God who "fills you with good" (103:5) or a God who will "fill us early with his lovingkindness" (90:14), but our passage returns to the Joban world. Psalm 123:3 is the only time in the Scripture where "full of contempt" appears (the word for contempt is *buz*, an easy-to-remember term). Not content with this uniqueness, our author also adds, twice, the concept of "great" fullness or "fully filled."

4 "Our soul is too much sated—with the scorning of those who are at ease, the contempt of the proud oppressors"

This verse begins with an unexpected verbal connection with the first Psalm of Ascent (Psalm 120). There the Psalmist lamented, "My soul has long dwelled" in words that are identical, except for the verb and the my/our, with 123:4, "our soul is much sated." Perhaps the verb changed from "dwelled" to "sated" because the Psalmist has changed his dwelling place between Psalm 120 and 123. Identical language encourages us to think of identical enemies, identical problems. Or, psychologically speaking, identical language means that the Psalmist hasn't left his memories behind. Though the liars and deceivers might be no longer in his life, they still claw at his soul. Why should that be the case? Why shouldn't one be able to divest the pain of one's memories as easily as one changes clothes? Memory both stabs and liberates but in this case the Psalmist seems to return to the stabbing memories.

Three words calling for more detailed consideration are "contempt" and "scorn" and "those at ease." "Contempt" and "scorn" are in poetic parallelism; in Hebrew they are *laag* and *buz*, and I kind of think of them as twins. Here come *laag* and *buz*, the Contempt Twins. Let's look at each. *Laag* appears as both a verb (19 times) and noun (6 times) in the Bible. I love the range of English words that is used to translate them: mock, deride, scorn, laugh to scorn, scoff. The most memorable biblical appearance for me of *laag* is in Job 21:3, where Job chides his friends, "Allow me to speak (literally, "lift me and I will speak") and, after I have spoken, mock on. . ." The verb *laag* only appears three times in Proverbs, but each time it hits us with a tsunami force. Wisdom "mocks" folly (1:26); "the one who mocks the poor holds his/

her maker in contempt" (17:5); "the eye that mocks one's father and scorns one's mother" will be picked out by the young eagles (30:17). The verbs "mock and despise/hold in contempt" (*laag, buz*) appear together in the last Proverbs passage, and they also appear together in Nehemiah 2:19, where Sanballet and Tobiah laughed at and despised the puny efforts of the returning Jews as they started to rebuild the temple. The noun form of "mockery" appears less frequently than its verb form, but in two places it appears not with *buz* with *qeles* (derision, Psalm 44:13; 79:4). Thus, we have a constellation of six words, both verbs and nouns, that capture the idea of derision or scorning or mocking or scoffing at or reproaching: *cherpah, buz, bazah* (the verb form of *buz*), *laag, laag, qeles*. Clearly the Psalmist has not fully been able to put his past behind him.

One other word that calls for mention is "ease." The phrase in 120:4 is "those who are at ease" (adjective is *shaanan*). Often its verbal form (*shaan*) is used in Scripture to capture a positive concept—those who dwell securely (Proverbs 1:33; Jeremiah 30:10; 46:27), but in several instances its noun form points to those who, because of what you might call 'too much' security have become lax and therefore ready for judgment. Most memorable is the familiar attack by Amos on the comfortable of Zion: "Woe to those who are at ease in Zion and trust in Mount Samaria" (using the adjective *shaanan*, Amos 6:1). *Shaanan* is also interesting because it enters into the verbal space of a concept that already has been twice introduced (122:6-7) to describe the desired goal of those who love Jerusalem—tranquility and peace. Though the words used in Psalm 122 are different (*shalah* and *shalvah*), they are close synonyms of *shaanan*.

It may be that "ease" is a double-edged sword. It is the goal of those who climb the mountains to Jerusalem (Psalm 122); it is also a characteristic of those who are oppress the Psalmist (Psalm 123). Just enough ease and tranquility enables peaceful and prosperous life but too much of that same ease can make us arrogant and over-confident. The author doesn't go as far as the author of Psalm 31:18 who, when also faced with lying lips (*siphthey sheqer*, the same phrase as in Ps 120:2), and with pride and contempt (*gaavah* and *buz*, very similar to the *gaayon* and *buz* in 123:4) wishes his opponents to be silenced. Here, our Psalmist is just fed up. Rather than being able to persist in the good feelings that filled Psalm 122, our author descends back to his "pre-journey" feelings. It will take more than wishing the bad memories away fully to enjoy the Heavenly City.

Psalm 124 A Song of Ascents. Of David.

1 If it had not been the Lord who was on our side
    —let Israel now say—
2 if it had not been the Lord who was on our side,
    when our enemies attacked us,
3 then they would have swallowed us up alive,
    when their anger was kindled against us;
4 then the flood would have swept us away,
    the torrent would have gone over us;
5 then over us would have gone
    the raging waters.
6 Blessed be the Lord,
    who has not given us
    as prey to their teeth.
7 We have escaped like a bird
    from the snare of the fowlers;
the snare is broken,
    and we have escaped.
8 Our help is in the name of the Lord,
    who made heaven and earth.

Psalm 124 in a Nutshell

Psalm 124 is a great Psalm of deliverance whose general or non-specific character makes it an appropriate song in settings as diverse as a national gatherings or personal triumphs. The generality of the language, rather than taking away from its potency, actually gives it a personal and historical resonance that encourages the reader to imagine times of personal danger and deliverance. Four images are used: those of swallowing, drowning or being washed away, being captured as a prey, and being released from a trap. They either relate to Israel's historical experience or point to experiences of threat faced by individuals. When studied in the context of our thesis about the Psalms of Ascent and its exploration of the levels of the spiritual life, we can see Psalm 124 functioning as a kind of counterbalance to Psalm 123. The difficult memories of 123 have, for the time being, been swallowed up in Psalm 124's confident and grateful expression of faith. These Psalms realistically capture the ebb and flow or pendulum swings of life's emotions. We look confidently to the one who is enthroned in the heavens; we plunge to our depths. This Psalm is a confident one.

1-5 "If not...then"

The Psalm's structure depends on these two temporal Hebrew words. A twofold *luley* ("if not/were it not") in verses 1 and 2 sets the conditions for the poem ("were it not the case that the Lord was on our side" in both vv 1, 2); then a three-fold *azay* ("then") in verses 3, 4, and 5 ("then swallowed," "then waters overwhelm," "then waters go over us") follows. You would think that this kind of construction would be very common in the Bible, but *luley* only appears a dozen times outside of this Psalm, such as in Genesis 31:42, "If (*luley*) the God of my father. . .had been with me, surely now (*kiy-attah*)..." or Genesis 43:10: "if (*luley*) we had not delayed, surely we would have returned by now (*kiy-attah*)." The word for "then" (*azay*) only appears in 124:3-5, but it easily can be seen as derived from the frequently-appearing *az*, "then, at that time."

Understanding the rhetorical structure of the first five verses of this psalm helps us not only grasp the flow of the words, but also emboldens us to use the same or other such structures in our own communication. We further note the repeated use of epanaphora in these verses. As we have seen, this device, which consist of repeating the first or several words of a verse in the next line or verse, helps to fix concepts in our mind. Ephanaphora says to us, so to speak, that the idea mentioned is not going to let us go easily. We have to "come back" to it. In this case the sad consequences of the Lord's *not* being with us/for us are stressed through this rhetorical device. Were the Lord not with us, then all kinds of difficult things would have come our way. This device actually lends an optimistic tone to Psalm 124, and thus provides a helpful and hopeful contrast to the almost desperate sense that life in the Holy City actually *could* be swallowed up by the machinations and scorn of proud and deceitful people (Psalm 123:4). Epanaphora is the literary mirror through which the Lord's saving activity on behalf of the people is reflected.

2 "Were not/had it not been the case that the Lord was for us—then when people rose up against us"

God's being "for" the people is expressed by means of that most simple of grammatical devices, the preposition and pronoun *lanu*, "to/for us." And the opposition against us is also expressed with the most common word *qum* ("to stand/rise up"). *Qum* appears more than 600 times and *adam* ("person/man") appears a like amount. Conflict happens; opposition develops in life. That is the common condition of humanity. Don't look at conflict, of "people rising up against you" as unusual. It happens. Know how to develop protective strategies to handle these situations. We probably need a book on that, too. . .

3 "Then alive we would have been swallowed up by their hot anger against us"

Though some scholars conflate this danger with the next (the overwhelming waters), I consider them separately, since each of the two is rooted in different experiences of the people of Israel. The combination of burning wrath and swallowing people points us in the direction of Korah's rebellion of Numbers 16. In that story, seared into the memory of Israel forever, one of the descendants of Levi had gathered a group of about 250 people who camped near him to protest the leadership of Moses and Aaron. Their allegation was that this duo had usurped too much power and was thereby lording authority over the people of Israel. The narrative doesn't want to create a forum to debate that issue but rather to *enhance* the authority of Moses and Aaron among the people. Predictably, Moses was angry, and he was angry with the verbal form of the word that matches our word in 124:3 (the verb is *charah*, "to be angry"): "And Moses was very angry" (Numbers 16:15). The punishment for Korah and his rebels was a unique one—being swallowed up alive by an earthquake. Let the cameras roll: "Then opened the earth its maw and swallowed them" (16:32); the passage goes on to detail all the things swallowed up by the earth, but our focus is just on the verb for "swallow": *bala*. Lest we forget that a swallowing is in view, the verb appears again in 16:34, giving us, along with 16:30, the thickest concentration of "swallowing" in the Bible.

And that this event reverberated through Israel's conscious-ness can be seen in the verb's appearance in reference to this event in Numbers 26:10 and Deuteronomy 11:6. As might be expected, that most psychologically deep book of the Bible, Job, picks up on the verb 7 times (e.g., 7:19; 10:18) and finds it useful to describe one of the painful ways his life might end. This verb, *bala*, and this noun, *charah*, that capture both the "swallowing" and "anger" of Numbers 16 is also present in Psalm 124:3. It is Korah's rebellion in one verse. Thus, the flow and tone of 124:3 is, 'Were the Lord not on our side, then we would have been like our forebears in Korah's rebellion—swallowed up alive, with our families and pos-sessions, wiped out from the earth.' It is a powerful way to apply the traditions of the people to the present reality.

4 "Then the waters would have overwhelmed us; the stream would have passed over our soul"

The suggestive phrase, "passed over our soul" reminds us that we are in the realm of tsunamis of the spirit and not Genesis 6, the Great Flood *redivivus*. The Scriptures know full well how to contrast gentle versus threatening waters. Isaiah 8:5-8 is a case in point. That author eloquently likens Israel's sidling up to unrighteous rulers as abandoning gently flowing waters only to be overwhelmed by the major floods of divine judgment. Specifically, the people, "refuse the waters of Shiloh, (waters that) flow gently." Yet, God will judge Israel—through the instrument of waters: "(God shall) overwhelm (with water) and pass over up to the neck," using the same two verbs (*shataph*, "overwhelm/engulf" and *abar*, "pass over") as in Ps 124:5. *shataph* and *abar* form a wonderful one-two punch to describe devastating and overwhelming waters.

The verb for "overwhelming" (*shataph*) has an interesting history. While other verbs were doing the hard labor of describing overwhelming waters of the great flood (Gen 6-8) or the waters that buried the Egyptian troops (Ex 14-15), *shataph* was not even a glint in anyone's eye. Yet when it appeared, in Leviticus, it had a gentler meaning—it was the word used to describe the priests' "rinsing" some of the sacred vessels (Lev 15:11, 12). And then Job got hold of it. Life turned topsy-turvy for Job; he repaid the favor by doing that with the Hebrew language. Note the intensity and hopelessness of this most beautiful author: "The waters wear away the stones; you overwhelm (verb is *shataph*) and wash away the after-growth of the dust of the earth; likewise the hope of people you destroy" (Job 14:19). Now *shataph* is placed squarely in connection with destructive activity. The divine waters wash away all hope just as they overwhelm the second growth or after-growth of the earth.

Thus, when the Psalmist speaks of his feet sinking deep in the mire, and his life thereby threatened with overwhelming waters, he finds it appropriate to refer to his experience with the verb *shataph* (Psalm 69:2, 15). A word that began its linguistic journey in the controlled environment of washing sacred vessels now has become a favorite to describe the feeling of being completely submerged by the waters. Thus we have the second danger facing the Psalmist if the Lord isn't on his side—the overwhelming waters.

5 "Then would have passed over our souls the proud waters"

As we just saw, verse 4, with its talk of overwhelming waters, can be quite daunting. Then, verse 5 repeats this thought, both as a way of reminding us of verse 4 and reliving the literary tension created by that verse. Here we have anadiplosis at work, the redoubling of a thought but in a situation where the *last* thought of a previous verse is the same as the *first* thought of the next. That is, "gone over our soul" both ends verse 4 and begins verse 5, with "proud waters" placed at the end of verse 5. And the phrase "proud waters" is unique in the Scripture; indeed *zeydon* ("proud/raging") is a *hapax legomenon*, though its meaning can be divined easily when you see the *zid* behind it. *Zid*, which means "proud/to be proud" in most of its biblical appearances, had its origin in cookery, where it meant to "boil" or "cook" something (e.g., the pottage Jacob cooked for Esau). As its meaning evolved, it changed from something "cooked" or something that "seethed" to someone that "acted proudly." The leap isn't as big as you might think.

Finally, when any student of the Bible hears the words "proud waters," Job 38 comes to mind. In that divine catechism of Job, God talks about creating the world and telling the ocean, "Here shall your proud waves be stayed" (38:11). Yet Job uses different words from Psalm 124 in his typically brilliant fashion. It is as if God is saying in Job, 'Your waves shall only come to right here; and your proud waves shall stay put here.' The word for "proud waves" is *ga'own gal,* a beautifully alliterative pair that one might call, with tongue firmly in check, "hubristic heaps."

6-7 "Blessed be the Lord, who had not given us over to be prey to their teeth. Our soul has escaped as a bird from the snare of the fowler"

Though two more perils are enumerated in these verses, the tone quickly changes. It is almost as if the Psalmist, upon narrating the deliverances in the "if not..then" clauses of verses 1-5, is convinced again that this is the way the Lord acts. God delivers from life-threatening perils. Thus, blessed be the Lord (v. 6). If God can deliver from the swallowing earth and overwhelming floods, God certainly can save from the predacious animals and the fowler's trap. The word for prey (*tereph*) allows us to enter into a memorable biblical verse that will aid us in learning the word. Its verbal form is *taraph,* which means "to tear/rend." Its first six appearances (total of 25 in the Bible) are in an interesting Hebrew grammatical construction where the verb is doubled as a way of intensifying meaning. Thus, Jacob laments, "Surely my son has been torn to pieces!" (Genesis 37:33; first two appearances of *taraph*; the identical thought is expressed in Genesis 44:28; the third pair is in Exodus 22:13). Thus you have mastered nearly 1/4 of the Biblical appearances of this word without really trying.

The more fascinating point of these verses, however, is the bird's escaping "from the fowler's trap." Rather than waxing eloquent on "timorous defenseless birds" that are "an apt emblem for helpless men," as one Victorian commentator did, we do better to see this phrase in connection with the tantalizing references to Psalm 91 which we have exposited in Psalm 121:6-8. The author of Psalm 121 had Psalm 91 "on the brain" during the climb to Zion, but really was in no position in that situation to exposit the perils with as much exhaustive fullness as did Psalm 91. Yet this phrase from Psalm 124 shows that our author has not forgotten that Psalm. It is as if Psalm 91 has a continuing presence in the Psalms of Ascent, defining the dangers and the deliverance of God. The first peril from which the fourfold-named God in Psalm 91 delivers the believer is called *mippach yaqush,* "the snare of the fowler." The phrase is identical to our phrase in Psalm 124, except that Psalm 124 uses the plural, "fowlers" while Psalm 91 uses the singular. We don't have many fowlers around today, except for my friend Chuck, and indeed the rather rare word might better be translated "trapper," but the meaning is the same. God not only delivers, but God does so in this verse in a way which takes us to the heart of one of the most beloved "deliverance" Psalms of them all.

8 "Our help is in the name of the Lord, who made heaven and earth"

Once deliverance is assured and order is restored, the Psalm ends. We have such an "orderly" ending to this Psalm that this verse has been used as a Call to Worship for those most "orderly and decent" Protestant religious bodies, the Presbyterian and Reformed. We have seen all these words previously. The "helper" is the same "helper" as in 121:1. The Lord who made "heaven and earth" is the same way that God's activity is described in Genesis 1:1 and many other places. Our author finally seems to be placing his foot down on heavenly *terra firma,* and we rejoice along with him. This is a fitting conclusion to the first third of the Psalms of Ascent. We started far off from any security, in isolation in Meshech and Kedar, facing the barbs and arrows of deceitful people. But then we began our journey, our Stairway to Heaven. We then arrived in the pleasant and comforting confines of Jerusalem. After admiring its appointments, we settled in for what we thought was going to be a life of peace and ease. Yet, old memories came back to haunt and harm, and Psalm 123 ended with uncertainty and a bit of desperation. Psalm 124 nicely remedies that, both with its engaging literary devices and reliance on deep historical traditions, and so by the end of this Psalm, as we wind up the first third of the Psalms of Ascent, we are on firm ground. Blessed be God. . .But then we recall that we are only one-third of the way along the journey.

Psalm 124 A Song of Ascents. Of David.

Notes

Psalm 125 A Song of Ascents.

1 Those who trust in the Lord are like Mount Zion,
   which cannot be moved, but abides forever.
2 As the mountains surround Jerusalem,
   so the Lord surrounds his people,
   from this time on and forevermore.
3 For the scepter of wickedness shall not rest
   on the land allotted to the righteous,
   so that the righteous might not stretch out
   their hands to do wrong.
4 Do good, O Lord, to those who are good,
   and to those who are upright in their hearts.
5 But those who turn aside to their own crooked ways
   the Lord will lead away with evildoers.
   Peace be upon Israel!

Psalm 125 in a Nutshell

Psalm 125 breathes a tone of quiet confidence and strength. The very security that the Psalmist so earnestly desired when he was far away from Zion, sojourning among deceivers in Meshech and Kedar (Psalm 120), is now part of his life. Yet, once his feet are firmly planted in the City of God, he realizes that there are still choices in life, choices to turn aside to "crooked ways" (v 5) or to be numbered among "the righteous" (v 3). At this stage of life in the Heavenly City, however, there is no struggle or conflict. He is not only having one very good day, but he realizes that it is possible for those who trust God to be so firmly and permanently fixed in trust as to become like the eternal Mount Zion itself (v 1). This, then, is a Psalm for those who are learning to live in trust and who realize that trusting God is the fundamental, good and anchoring principle of life.

1 "Those who trust in the Lord are as firm as Mount Zion, which doesn't totter but which lasts forever"

This verse picks up where 124:8 left us. Once the author realizes that the four scourges of that Psalm (earthquake swallowing, waters overwhelming, teeth ripping, snare trapping) no longer threaten, the Psalmist here begins to use language of confidence and stability, of solidity and firmness. Three verbs in the first verse of Psalm 125 capture that growing feeling of security, verbs I have translated "trust, totter, last." Each invites brief consideration. Though *batach* ("trust") appears 120 times in the Bible, more than one-third of these appearances are in the Psalms alone. If you want to learn about trusting God, then, the Psalms is the quintessential book to read. You can't get very far in life if you don't trust others (sometimes selectively, of course); the Psalmist is convinced that the same principle is true in the spiritual realm. Normally the verb is only used once in a Psalm, but on rare occasions, where there is what you might call a "trust chorus" (Psalm 115:8-11) or where the rhythms of the Psalm are structured around the word (Psalm 56), the word is repeatedly used.

Psalm 22 presents what I call the Biblical "struggle for trust." This Psalm, recited so movingly by Christ on the cross, poses the question of whether trusting God is really worth it. In Psalm 22 the author, suffering so greatly, being mocked by tormenters, is confronted by the reality of stories of God's past deliverance, and he faces a dilemma. Do you continue to trust when truly in need? The word *batach* washes over us in that Psalm. Our ancestors trusted in you (*batchu*, 22:4 (English/v 5 Hebrew; the subsequent references are all to the English text). They trusted (*batchu*, again, v 4) and you delivered them (using *palath* rather than the expected *natsal*). Lest we miss the flow, the next verse says how they "trusted" (*batchu* again, v 5) and were not put to shame.

That issue of trust, then, becomes the crucial issue, the nub, of Psalm 22. Why? Because the scoffers stand around and mockingly repeat the thought,

"He trusted in God (v 8, using the different but visually evocative word for trust *galal* —literally "to roll away" or, metaphorically, to "commit one's way"); let God deliver him if God really delights in him."

Wrestling with this dilemma, then, the Psalmist affirms that trust is the route he will go in the next verse. It literally says,

"You are the one who made me trust (verb is *batach)* upon the breasts of my mother " (v 9).

Trust wins in Psalm 22, and this lesson might be in the deep background of the Psalmist's hopeful confession in Psalm 125.

The trusting person will not "totter" (verb is *mot).* If the Psalms have a near 'controlling interest' in the word for trust, they absolutely dominate the market on *mot,* "tottering" (nearly two-thirds of the 38 occurrences in the Psalms). The chorus of affirmations of the Psalmist, who will not be "shaken," appear over and over (Psalm 15:5; 16:8; 21:7; 30: 6, etc.). An interesting play on the word occurs in Psalm 46, where the mountains may "shake" or "slip" or "totter" (*mot* is verb, v 2) into the heart of the sea, but the one who trust in God will not be "moved" or "shaken" or "totter" (*mot* is verb, v 5). In fact, Psalm 46 very consciously is "playing" with the word and a similar-sounding *mur* ("to change"). The words that are translated so majestically, and somewhat verbosely, in the King James English as "though the earth be removed, and though the mountains be carried. . ." (v. 2) are, in the Hebrew, simply, *mur* and *mot.* Though Psalm 46 says that the believer's security even exceeds that of the mountains, Psalm 125 is content enough with likening our security to Mount Zion. Finally, Mount Zion "lasts" forever (using the common verb *yashab,* "to sit"). Mount Zion just "sits there," as immovable as anything one might imagine. To live in this kind of trust so that one isn't moved, so that one sits securely as the everlasting mountain, is a bit of a dream (a concept which begins the next Psalm), but it is the world in which the Psalmist now lives. His help is in the name of the Lord (124:8). His security is affirmed (125:1). But still life goes on.

2 "As the mountains surround Jerusalem, so the Lord surrounds His people, now and forever"

The theme of security continues, again using a word (*sabib*, "around, surround") that occurs hundreds of times in the Bible. God's presence is likened to the enveloping necklace of mountains around Jerusalem. Three verses in a row stress the Psalmist's calm security! This threefold chain won't easily be broken.

3 "Because the rod/scepter of the wicked shall not rest/settle down upon the lot of the righteous; so that the righteous don't send out their hands out with evil"

This is a strange verse, the rough edges of which commentators and translators have been trying to smooth out for millennia. Unusual phrases and words used in unusual ways fill this verse. *Shebet* can mean either "scepter" (a sign of authority) or, more frequently, "tribe," such as a tribe of Israel. The most famous use of it in the former way is in Genesis 49:10, which talks about the "scepter" (of authority) not departing from Judah. Psalm 125:3 is the only reference to the "scepter of wickedness/the wicked" in the Bible. The word "wicked" probably points to a wicked ruler or opponent, and not to the wicked in general, but that is speculative. The verb that describes the scepter's activity is also strange: *yanuach*, "to rest" (verb is *nuach*). Used first to describe the positioning of the ark on dry land ("it rested"—Genesis 8:4), it normally refers to the Lord's giving "rest" from enemies (Deuteronomy, Joshua several places) or the Spirit of the Lord "resting" on people (Numbers 11, etc.). Usually when you see *nuach* as you are reading, you heave a sigh of relief and say, "Hmm, things are going to calm down now." But here we have the possibility of an "evil" scepter "resting" on good people. Yet we are comforted to see that it *won't* rest on them. It won't rest on their "lot" (*goral*) which is understandable but again a rather unique way of saying it.

Finally, the righteous don't stretch out/send their hands to evil or with evil. The connecting word *lemaan*, "so that," gives a reason for the preceding. Because the scepter of wicked rulers doesn't settle on the righteous, the righteous don't send out their own hands to do evil. Would that suggest the reverse is true? That the righteous would be tempted to evil if the scepter of the wicked settled down on them? The thought isn't clearly or convincingly expressed. It almost seems as if the Psalmist "borrowed" the thought in the second half of the verses from some writing primer, where students are given words to put together to make up a sentence that makes some sense, but the purpose of the exercise is just to develop greater verbal facility and a greater variety of words. This is certainly not the first verse in the Bible that doesn't "ring" with great power (see my exposition of Jonah 2:9, in *Something Fishy*).

4-5 "Do good, O Lord, to the good, that is to the upright in heart. But to those who incline towards the roundabout or crooked ways, well, the Lord will make them walk away with the doers of evil. Peace be on Israel"

The words for "righteous" (*tsadiq*), "upright" (*yashar*) and "good" (*tob*) all occupy the same meaning universe, and they are no doubt used interchangeably here and in the previous verse ("righteous" only occurs in v 3). We are not given a description of their lives or their conduct; it seems to be clear who they are. Very few authors who write about the "righteous" or the "upright" or the "good" see themselves as not among that company. Whereas the words to describe those who are good are relatively few in Hebrew, words proliferate for describing the bad guys. I think that is a general phenomenon of language and the reality of life.

Books are generally written by those who feel themselves either morally good or who believe they have special insight into some aspect of life. They spend time differentiating themselves from others. Often these 'others' have to be characterized in ways that emphasize their difference or their "badness." Suffice it to say that in these Psalms we have so far seen liars, those who deceive, evil people, those who work injustice, those who do bad things. On the other hand, however, we have the good or righteous or upright. The linguistic world is already tipping with more words for the bad guys. Now, instead of "evil" people, we have yet another concept: those who follow a "crooked" path. That word for "crooked," *aqalqal,* only occurs twice in the Bible, and in the other instance it also appears in a poetic context and is best trans-lated "roundabout" or even "remote" (Jud 5:6). The underlying verb is *aqal,* itself a *hapax,* which means "to twist" or "pervert." In Haggai 1:4 it is used to describe "perverted" justice. Thus, when we return to our context we recognize a word that takes us on a twisting journey, in contrast to those on the "straight" or "right" path (*yashar*). It's interesting that Proverbs, which has a pretty rich language of foolishness and sluggardy, which commends the straight path, doesn't pick up on this word for crookedness.

So, this word for "crooked" is rare, but their activity in verse 5 is pretty common—they "turn aside." Life in the Scriptures is often likened to a path; here the people obviously are going "off path." It was only in late twentieth-century America that those who chose "alternative" or "crooked" paths were held up as worthy of imitation. But this comment brings up the theological point of some interest: if the Bible holds that the "straight" path is one that is to be followed, but our culture increasingly wants to explore life "off the path," and encourage people to do so, how does one connect the freedom of going "off path" with the bib-lical focus of staying "on path?"

The hope of the Psalmist is that God will make these people "walk" (the very common word) along with other "doers of evil/

iniquity." The words for "do" (*paal*), along with "create" (*bara*) and "make/do" (*asah*) occupy the field of major verbs of "doing" in Biblical Hebrew; *aven* (78x) is a similarly common word for "trouble, misfortune, evil." And, we finally return to linguistic solid ground when we realize that the phrase "workers of evil" or "doers of iniquity" is also used elsewhere in the Bible: For example, Psalm 6:8 says: "turn away from me (using a different verb than in 125:5) all you who work evil." The Psalmist has now departed from his little linguistic frolic of verse 3 and brought us safely to the verbal confines of traditional speech. The security that he longs for in 125:1 is now reflected in his words. "Peace be upon Israel," is a great way, then, to end the Psalm. We are in a stable place, with the Lord surrounding us. Life in this Holy City is really not so bad. And, if we keep reading, we will see that satisfaction will turn to joy in the next Psalm.

Psalm 126 A Song of Ascents.

1 When the Lord restored the fortunes of Zion,
    we were like those who dream.
2 Then our mouth was filled with laughter,
    and our tongue with shouts of joy;
    then it was said among the nations,
    "The Lord has done great things for them."
3 The Lord has done great things for us,
    and we rejoiced.
4 Restore our fortunes, O Lord,
    like the watercourses in the Negeb.
5 May those who sow in tears
    reap with shouts of joy.
6 Those who go out weeping,
    bearing the seed for sowing,
    shall come home with shouts of joy,
    carrying their sheaves.

Psalm 126 in a Nutshell

This Psalm can neatly be divided into two equal sections: verses 1-3 and 4-6. The first part uses vivid language to capture the over-mastering joy of those who have returned to the Holy City; the second part expresses a longing for this joy to continue, even amid the new reversal of fortunes that people face. The specific event that may be in the background of this Psalm is the return of exiles from the Babylonian captivity in the mid sixth-century BCE. My argument is that this historical moment gave birth to a feeling and perspective that became loosed from that event and was then applied both to later national experiences of joy as well as individual rejoicing. It is not at all unusual for the memorials or events of our national life to give shape to our individual longings and self-definition. A national holiday becomes celebrated in a unique way in each family that observes it. The national word "freedom," so precious in America and celebrated on July 4, becomes expressed in countless acts of individual "freedom" that differ widely from each other. The exultant joy felt by returning exiles is almost tele-pathically or, theologically speaking, divinely transmitted from national experience to individual life and, consistently with my argument here, to those on pilgrimage to Jerusalem.

1 "When the Lord turned back the (great) turning/captivity, it was as if we were dreamers"

In keeping with the theme of this book, the memory of return from exile then becomes an important memory for those who are making or have just completed their Stairway to Heaven, their Journey to Jerusalem. But we will see as this Psalm progresses that too much joy too early in the new life almost invariably produces its opposite. Though one would like grace alone to be determinative of the new life--the life after the Journey to Jerusalem--the stark reality is that *real* life impinges upon that *new* life. Alternatively said, nature catches up to grace and, sadly it seems, may have the last word or, as here, the penultimate word. If the Christian can sing: "bane and blessing, pain and pleasure, by the cross are sanctified," the author of Psalm 126 could also say that joy and distress are both part of the new life in the City of God.

But before we get ahead of ourselves, let's just stop for a moment to focus on the journey so far. Note the progression of emotions as the Psalms of Ascent unfold. Distress and even disgust captures us in the Kedar's and Meshech's of life (Psalm 120). Great yearning characterizes the beginning of the journey (Psalm 121). Gladness is felt upon first arriving in the city (Psalm 122); dependence on God is quickly mentioned (Psalm 123); God's deliverance from all foes is acknowledged (Psalm 124); satisfaction at all these things is then expressed (Psalm 125). Now, with the full realization of the wondrous new life of the people of God and of the individual who has made the journey, joy rules (Psalm 126). It is as if the emotional temperature "climbs" as the reality of the new life in the Heavenly City dawns more and more on the faithful believer.

We will get to the words for "joy" in verses 2-3, but here the Psalm first lays out the reasons for joy: the return from captivity. The words are suggestive: literally it is, "In God's returning the return." The middle word of the verse, *shibath,* is a biblical *hapax legomenon* but is easily recognizable from its more frequently-occurring cousin *shebuth* or *shibyah,* usually translated "captivity." It is as if the delirium of joy felt by the author in the first three verses has given him a temporary case of divine dyslexia or verbal inventiveness. The alliteration of "returning the return" is not lost on readers of Hebrew. *Shub/shib* ("returning the return") is the action here. The phrase also appears in Psalm 85:1 and Job 42:10, among other places.

The result is that "we became like dreamers." Biblical Hebrew uses two nearly identical words for "dream." The verb is *chalam*; the noun is *chalom.* The former appears here, "as those who dream." Together the noun and verb occur more than ninety times in the Bible but, fascinatingly enough, almost fifty of them are in the book of Genesis alone. Genesis is our "book of dreams." Though God caused "deep sleep" to fall upon Abram, he is never said to have dreamed. The first one who does so in the Bible is a non-Israelite—Abimelech (Genesis 20: 3). Yet the word is seemingly reserved for Joseph and his oneiromantic activity. He has skill in interpreting dreams, a divine gift that gets him out of a real jam at Pharaoh's court and propels him to the lofty heights of Pharaonic administration. Yet, the noun form of the word was also used pejoratively by Joseph's brothers before they decided to toss him in the pit: here comes that dreamer! (*baal hachalomoth,* literally "the Lord of the dreams"). Rather than seeing the author of Psalm 126 attributing special divine skills in oneiromancy to those who have returned from captivity, we are on firmer ground if we recognize that the exultation of those returning was as if they were living in a dream world. That this is along the right track is confirmed by verses 2 and 3.

2-3 "Then our mouths were filled with laughter and our tongues with shouts of joy. Then the people of other nations said, 'The Lord has done great things with these (folk).' Yes, the Lord has done great things with us; we are overjoyed"

Our author uses three different words to capture the faces of joy that fill the hearts and that empower the voice to sing these words. In addition, the author pulls out all the literary stops by combining ephanaphora and anadiplosis in consecutive verses; the repetition of *az* is an example of the former, while the almost perfectly redoubled "The Lord has done great things" illustrates the latter. The effect on reader is to invite us into the joy felt by the returned exiles, by those who have climbed the Stairway to Heaven. What makes these two verses even more potent is that the first recognition of the "great things" done by God for the people of God is by "the nations" and not the people of God themselves. I can just see the huddled crowds of far-off peoples, witnessing the joyous parade of returning exiles, and saying, "Wow, this is *some* party! Their God must have done some pretty great things." Since joy is the tone of these verses, it is best that we learn the three words: *sechoq* ("laughter"), *rinnah* ("shout of joy"), and *sameach* ("glad/joyful/merry").

People who laugh in Scripture do it for a number of reasons; the laugh itself may not tell you much. There are laughs of derision and scorn (Psalm 2:4); there is the laughter that arises from making a joke of someone (Job 12:4); Jeremiah complains about becoming a laughingstock (20:7), as does Job (12:1-4); Proverbs can even say that doing harm to others is "laughter" to a fool (Proverbs 10:23), a thought echoed by Ecclesiastes, who talks about the laughter of the fool (Ecclesiastes 7:6). A related and almost identical word *tsachaq* makes its entrance in Genesis and then almost completely disappears there, and thereafter the abrasive sound of the initial *tsade* is replaced by the much more mollient *sa/se* of our word (*sechoq*).

Context, therefore, is king in determining the "tone" of the laughter. Here we have laughter of unexampled joy. The three-fold appearance of *rinnah* ("joyful shout," vv 2, 5, 6) seals the deal. *Rinnah,* and its related verbal form *ranan,* basically mean "to give a ringing cry," or "to shout," but by the time one gets to the Psalms, where these words primarily choose to reside, we have one predominant meaning: to shout for joy. One can "sing" for joy (51:14), "shout" for joy (35:27), "greatly rejoice" (71:23) or "rejoice" or "shout." The sound is, no doubt, the same in all instances. Even Job, that most querulous and murmurant sufferer, uses the word twice to mean "shout of joy" (29:13; 38:7). Thus, we can have no doubt; the three-fold appearance of *rinnah* in Psalm 126 bends the "laughter" of verse 2 in the direction of extremely joyous laughter. And, if doubt remained, the final word of verse 3 confirms our approach. Though *sameach,* "joy/merry/glad" appears only one-third as often as its noun cousin *simchah* and only one-fifth as often as the verb *samach* ("rejoice, be glad), its meaning in Psalm 126:3 is clear beyond peradventure. We have the return of the exiles; and their hearts are filled with joy. We have the "return" of the soul that had wandered into and lived in the vale of Meshech and Kedar. Now it is comfortably settled in the Heavenly Jerusalem. Gladness reigns. For a while. . .

4 "Turn, O Lord, our captivity (again) like the wadis of the Negeb"

I translated the verse literally. A more "user-friendly" translation might be, "Restore our fortunes again, O Lord, as the streams of the south are replenished." We see that not all is at peace in Zion. . .*again.* We recall that there was a return of the stabbing memories (of Psalm 120) in Psalm 123, but the Psalmist deftly dealt with them through the potent affirmations of Psalm 124; now we have new concerns. But we are not brought into the details or heart of the complaint. The author simply wants *another* turning, *another* return from captivity, *another* heady parade back to the Holy Land. The spiritual life is like that. Once you have

had the initial surge of joy in faith, you want it to return, especially when you encounter mammoth obstacles. You cling to that
experience of joy as if it had talismanic power or an apotropaic
force. You so much want to repeat it. The Psalmist does, too, and
this time he points to the dry wadis in the desiccated south for
an illustration. They are bone dry one moment and then surging
the next after a refreshing and sudden rain. 'Please, O God,' the
Psalmist intones, 'restore us like those streams!'

Something has knocked the Psalmist off the calm center of
confident faith of Psalm 124:8-125:2, and he longs for restoration.
It is sort of an unrealistic expectation, to be sure, always to be
on the mountain top. But here, with the reference to the wadis,
the impression given is that life is either bone dry or rushing with
water. Then, the Psalmist ponders. . . Perhaps a restoration like a
gradually growing corn crop would have been better (an image he
immediately develops).

**5-6 "Those sowing in tears will reap in joy. Again, if they go forth with
weeping, they shall certainly bring in their seed, coming with rejoicing,
bringing in the sheaves"**

As if on cue, the Psalmist changes the image of restoration from
the quickly restored wadi to that of a gradually-growing crop. In
addition, he eschews anadiplosis for a reiteration of concepts with
different words. That is, we have "sowing in tears" and "going
forth with weeping." The Psalmist's hope now is in the gradual
restoration of fortunes, the "little-by-little" progress in faith.
There are several disappointments and restorations between the
sowing and the reaping, but those who sow in tears (i.e, those
facing the new but undefined challenges of the life of faith) will
certainly experience a joyous harvest. The return of *rinnah* means
that our shout of joy in the initial surge of joy in verse 2 will
be repeated. As if to drive home the point, the author repeats
himself in verse 6. They go forth in tears, bearing the asperities

of current life, but they will no doubt reap the harvest of joy, bringing sheaves with them.

We only want to pause for a moment because of rare words used to describe the harvest process. The verb for reaping, *qatsar*, to be sure, is common, but the way in which the sowing takes place in verse 6, and the sheaves that are bound, are both expressed in rare ways.

Those who sow are said to "bear precious seed," and the one who reaps is said to "bear his sheaves." No one quite knows what to do with the *meshek* in the middle between "bearing" and "seeds." The word only occurs twice in the Bible and its other appearance, in the difficult verbal netherworld of Job, is less than pellucid. So, scholars guess. One guess is "precious" so that one has "precious seed." Another says that the one sowing bears "the measure of seed." Another rendering of *meshek* is "a bag," so it becomes "a bag of seed." Another just punts and says "carrying seed to sow." The verbal form of the word is *mashak*, a rather common verb trans-lated "do draw" or "to drag." A memorable appearance of it is in Genesis 37:28, where it is used to describe the action of Midianite traders, who "dragged" Joseph out of the pit. But "bearing drag-ging seed" doesn't read very well. So, one might do well to say, "bearing and dragging the seed along. . ." though we really don't know. Then, there is the meaning of *alummah*, the last word of the verse. All translations go with "sheaves," even though there is only one other place (Genesis 37, though many places in that chapters) where it appears. You bear seed (maybe you "drag" it too); you bring sheaves home. That will be the new rhythm that the Psalmist suggests for the spiritual life. It is a very wise devel-opment here. Don't look for the overflowing wadis; rather, look for the gradually-growing sheaves and then, at the appropriate time, harvest them. *That* will be your key, the new key for living in the City of God.

I can't end these thoughts without a personal story which brings home how foreign the agricultural world assumed by the

Scriptures is to us. One of the great old Gospel Hymns, based on Psalm 126:6 is "Bringing in the Sheaves." You can look up the words, but the joyous chorus is "Bringing in the sheaves, bringing in the sheaves. We will go rejoicing, bringing in the sheaves. . ." My Evangelical nurture after I moved to the San Francisco Bay Area in 1967 assured that I mastered dozens of mellifluous Gospel hymns, including this one. My brother, eight years my junior, learned even more. He started learning them when he was still 8 or 9 years old. One day, while singing this chorus next to him in a packed church, I heard him sing with full-throated fervor, "Bringing in the cheese, bringing in the cheese. We will go rejoicing, bringing in the cheese." Now, *that's* what suburban living does to you. . .

Notes

_____

_____

_____

_____

_____

_____

_____

_____

_____

_____

_____

_____

_____

_____

_____

_____

_____

_____

_____

_____

_____

_____

Psalm 127 A Song of Ascents. Of Solomon.

1 Unless the Lord builds the house,
  those who build it labor in vain.
Unless the Lord guards the city,
  the guard keeps watch in vain.
2 It is in vain that you rise up early
  and go late to rest,
eating the bread of anxious toil;
  for he gives sleep to his beloved.
3 Sons are indeed a heritage from the Lord,
  the fruit of the womb a reward.
4 Like arrows in the hand of a warrior
  are the sons of one's youth.
5 Happy is the man who has
  his quiver full of them.
He shall not be put to shame
  when he speaks with his enemies in the gate.

Psalm 127 in a Nutshell

We have been tracing the movements of those who have arrived in the Holy City after the arduous pilgrimage climb of Psalm 121. They arrived in Psalm 122 and then got their bearings. The quest of the next four Psalms was first for stability (123-124), then satisfaction (125) and then joy (126). Now, having rooted ourselves deeply in faith, and recognized the satisfactions it yields and the joys it brings, we are ready to explore the theme of fruitfulness. This is sort of the divine equivalent of Maslow's Hierarchy of Needs. Indeed, Maslow ought to be accorded recognition not so much because he "discovered" a very useful system of describing stages of human motivation but because he "recognized" something that was already "discovered" thousands of years previously in the flow of the Psalms of Ascent. In Psalm 127 we have the results of what might call "settling into faith." Settling into faith means that you have a sense of security and belongingness. But eventually your goal is production or fruitfulness. Here, and in the next Psalm, that "production" is connected with bearing children, but any kind of fruitfulness will do. We long for productivity and the Psalm encourages us in that longing.

1 "If the Lord will not build the house, in vain do those who work at building it work;
If the Lord doesn't watch the city, in vain do those who watch it watch"

I have put these half-verses atop and abottom (new word, my own coinage). Note the way we usually describe this is to say that the verses are "atop (of) each other" but, in fact, they aren't atop each other. The one on the bottom stays on the bottom. So, we need a phrase such as I have given us to illustrate their parallelism. We are "building a house" and "watching a city," two important elements in providing security, which is the basis of fruitfulness in verses 3-5. We know of course that it is the Lord who is building the house and watching the city, though this reality doesn't eliminate the need for human builders and human watchers. The Psalm is the only one of this collection said to be "of Solomon," and that makes sense, since Solomon is the quintessential builder in Israel—the builder of a kingdom, the builder of the House of God.

Two points for people of faith that emerge from this verse ought not to be missed: 1) That the true foundation even of tasks that are most clearly performed by people is the Lord; and 2) That cultivation of the basic elements of security (building houses/setting up a city watch) is the prerequisite for fruitfulness (vv 3-5). A word on each. There is no statement more obvious that in order to build a house and, especially to build the Temple of Jerusalem, an order had to be placed with Hiram of Tyre to cut down trees and then place them on boats, and then sail them down to Israel, where they were hauled overland to build the temple. One needed tools and equipment and people. No doubt there were complaints about working conditions and safety. Not having an "Israelite OSHA" to enforce safe working conditions meant that builders may have fallen from parapets or been on the receiving end of an errant hammer or axe blade inadvertently flying off the handle. Covering all this messiness and the long duration of the building process in one elegant phrase, the Psalmist confidently asserts that the Lord is the one actually building the house. Should the workers feel slighted for not being recognized? Not in the least. Should they desire to be called "co-creators" with God of the temple? Certainly people need their recognition for work done, and there was no doubt a temple banquet for that, but here the emphasis is on God's actual building of it. So many things can go wrong in any human endeavor of consequence that it is a proper and spiritually healthy thing to do to recognize the centrality of the divine role in all important, as well as more mundane, human tasks.

The vocabulary of "building" in this verse is both standard and arresting. The first clause uses the standard word for "building," while the second clause uses two words "in vain" (*shav*) and "labor"(verb is *amal*) that make us pause. The "vanity" of which this verse speaks was first mentioned in Exodus 20 in connection with taking the Lord's name "in vain" in the Ten Commandments (Exodus 20:7). Thus, we see that the original meaning of the term is not to be found in "cursing" (i.e., don't say "God damn!" Or worse. . .) but in considering God's name, and thus God's power, ineffectual. Building a house is ineffectual unless one recognizes that the true builder is God. Though the foundations may seem firm, they really are flimsy. The second word, translated "labor" or "toil" (to differentiate it from the more common verbs for "build" or "work"), is especially noteworthy because eight of its eleven appearances are in Ecclesiastes. In that book it is the "fruitlessness of labor/toil" which the author laments (e.g, 1:3; 2: 11, 19, 20, etc.). Thus, by using the verb *amal* at the end of the first clause, the author is "winking" at us, not just saying explicitly that the Lord's help in building the city is (ahem) foundational, but that if we don't have that building power, then our "toil" is "vain." If we don't recognize the Lord's action in the labor of building a house, then one might enter into Ecclesiastes' despair. The same can be said, much more briefly, about watching the city.

Familiar words appear in the first half of the half-verse, but then "vanity" (*shav* again) and "watching" (*shaqad*) are in the second part. *Shaqad* is a specialized word (appearing a dozen times in the Bible) for the action of intense observation. This action can be attributed either to God or humans. Its most memorable appearance outside Psalm 127:1 is in Jeremiah 1, where God uses a play on words to show that God is "watching over" the divine word (*shaqad*, 1:12). Jeremiah thereafter becomes so enamored of the word that he uses it four other times, having a near controlling interest in the term.

2 "Vain it is that you rise early and stay up real late if all you do is eat the bread of pain, because he gives sleep to the beloved"

For the third time in two verses, vanity appears (*shav* again). Though the Psalmist uses a somewhat rare word for useless toil in verse 1, a word that is "owned" by Ecclesiastes (*amal*), he uses a different word than Ecclesiastes for vanity (that author uses *hebel*). More than half of the 73 appearances of *hebel* ("vanity") in the Bible are in Ecclesiastes, though he never once uses the Psalmist's word for vanity. Yet our vanity continues, but now in a much more intimate way. One might look at 127:1 as displays of public vanity (without the Lord's help) whereas 127:2 describe instances of private vanity. It is likewise ineffectual for us to get up early and stay up late, slaving away all the time. The implication is that unless the Lord "works" for us, it is just painful and useless work. In this case the word for painful labor is *etseb* which only appears seven times in the Bible, but its first occurrence is so vivid that we never forget it. It is the word used for Eve's "pain in childbearing" of Genesis 3:16. The verse thus teaches us that all our "childbearing" labor is in vain (the unstated message is that it is in vain unless the Lord helps).

Rather than saying explicitly "unless the Lord builds," it says "for he gives sleep to his beloved." It is a curious but endearing phrase. What is *not* said is the obverse: that God gives "success" to those who work hard and realize that God is behind their work.

What *is* said is that God gives them rest. This is not the same word for rest or sleep used to describe Jonah's deep swoon (Jonah 1:5), but is rather the common word for it *(shenah)*. But the unusual word is "to his beloved." It is unexpected because the language of intimacy has, so far, been rather lacking in the Psalms of Ascent. There is security and satisfaction and even joy but, so far, there has not been much emphasis on the unity and connectedness of the people of God. The word "beloved" *(yadid)* is rare in the Bible (nine occurrences), and its most memorable appearance is its two-fold use in Isaiah's song of the vineyard of Isaiah 5 (twice in v 1). In that verse, somewhat freely translated, "Let me sing a song for the one I love. . .My beloved. . .," Israel is likened to God's vineyard that becomes overgrown with weeds and ultimately has to be torn up. Yet, the pathos of that passage is increased because of the little word *yadid.* So it is in Psalm 127:2. "God gives sleep to the beloved." Perhaps that is what the beloved ones of God really need—not success but sleep. Sleep on that one.

3-4 "Indeed, an inheritance from the Lord are one's sons (and daughters). They are wages, the fruit of the womb. As are arrows in the hand of a mighty man, so are the sons (children) of one's youth"

Now that intimacy has been gently probed through the word *yadid,* we turn to fruitfulness. The "fruit" of intimacy is children. They are even called here the "fruit" *(peri)* of the womb. Once the reader is convinced that it is the Lord who stands behind the success of every meaningful human venture, we are ready to consider the idea of fruitfulness. But there are two little words that arrest our attention, *sakar* and *chets.* Almost every translation renders the former as "reward," and indeed it may be so translated here, but of the 28 appearances of it in the Bible, about 25 are best translated "wages" or "hire." The verb form *sakar* is the common word for "hiring" someone to do a task. Looking at children as "wages" rather than a "reward" or "prize" or "gift" is jarring at first. Our first reaction is, 'How can those precious little additions to our family be *anything else* but a sort of divine reward or gift?'

But when we remember we are in the world of building and watchmen of verse 1, we can understand the concept of "wages" more easily than "reward." This Psalm is about working and the results of work. To see that same concept operating in verse 3 is not exceptional. The children are a payment of sorts, perhaps a downpayment on the next generation. Then, children are likened to arrows (*chets*) in the hands of a mighty man. The image is apt, since arrows were earlier used (Psalm 120) as in instrument of vengeance. Now, it is as if the image is "replaced" by one of arrows as blessing, or something that comes as a result of labor. Ideally, old animosities are replaced in the Heavenly City as one learns to be steadfast, joyful and fruitful. The arrows are now not sharpened to aim at other people; they are likened to the blessing of children.

One brief note. The word for children in verses 3 and 4 is *banim,* literally "sons." I fudged a bit in my translation by adding "daughters." One might say that the notion of daughters is already included in the ancient concept of "sons" but, then again, the Scriptures know how to enumerate sons *and* daughters when it wants to (see, e.g., Job 1:1-5). The picture here is of sons who stand with the father to defend the family at the gate of the town. My addition of the word "daughters" is a concession to modern sensibilities—not to mention also that I have a daughter upon whom I am, at times, greatly reliant.

5 "Blessed is the mighty man who has his quiver full of them! Such people won't be put to shame when they speak with their enemies in the gate"

The image of warrior with arrows continues. Now the children, his arrows, are placed in the quiver. The connection between a full quiver and warding off shame is the theme of the rest of the verse; and the connection isn't hard to see. A full quiver of arrows enables protection and security. One isn't put to shame. The first use of the word "shame" in the Scriptures is its most vivid: in the Garden of Eden, before sin entered, the man and his wife were both naked and not ashamed (*bosh* is verb, Genesis 2:25). We have thus seen two instances in this brief Psalm of words selected that have a powerful appearance in Genesis 1-3 (childbirth and shame). Perhaps the Psalms of Ascent have more of a (re)creating function than previously thought. But security is the last word of this Psalm, security at the gate for those who have climbed the Stairway to Heaven.

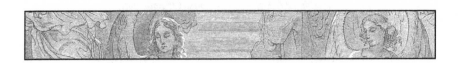

Psalm 128 A Song of Ascents.

1 Happy is everyone who fears the Lord,
   who walks in his ways.
2 You shall eat the fruit of the labor of your hands;
   you shall be happy, and it shall go well with you.
3 Your wife will be like a fruitful vine
   within your house;
   your children will be like olive shoots
   around your table.
4 Thus shall the man be blessed
   who fears the Lord.
5 The Lord bless you from Zion.
   May you see the prosperity of Jerusalem
   all the days of your life.
6 May you see your children's children.
   Peace be upon Israel!

Psalm 128 in a Nutshell

Were you to take a random sample of a hundred diligent Bible students, I dare say that this Psalm would not make it into a list of top ten Psalms for any of them. Or maybe even their top twenty-five Psalms. Yet once we see it in its organic connection to the rest of the Psalms of Ascent and its position in this collection, the Psalm comes alive. It continues the theme of fruitfulness, developed so nicely in Psalm 127; it provides a helpful corrective to the "worthless toil" noted in Psalm 127:2 by talking about happiness of eating from the toil of one's hands (128:1-2). But it also continues the theme of fruitfulness from the preceding Psalm by adding a dimension of deep familial satisfaction to our growing collection of joys in the City of God. Thus, the life in the City of God yields steadfastness, satisfaction, joy, fruitfulness and now a fruitful and joyful family. It seems that even though we have stopped "climbing" the hills to Jerusalem, we keep "climbing" emotionally and spiritually as we continue our life in the Holy City.

1 "Blessed are all who fear the Lord, who walk in his ways"

This verse is both familiar and strange: its familiarity is clear because it presents themes that resonate with any reader of the Psalms and the Bible in general. Yet the words introducing these themes are, except for one reference, otherwise foreign to the Psalms of Ascent. The first word, for example, *esher* ("happiness/blessedness") occurs forty-five times in the Bible (twenty-five of which are in the Psalms), but its only other appearance in the Psalms of Ascent is in the previous verses, 127:5. One would have expected its more frequent appearance in these Psalms. It is the first word of the first Psalm; one might even say that the prominence of its location in the Psalter (in 1:1) is an indication that blessedness not only follows for the reader of Psalm 1 but for the entire collection. The Psalter is baptized in blessedness. "Blessedness" is the "Title" of the Psalms. Run the Psalms through your mind: "Blessed is the one who trusts in Him" (2:12); "Blessed is the one whose sin is covered" (32:1); "Blessed is the nation whose God is the Lord" (33:12). We could go on for some time. Strange it is, then, that we rarely encounter it in the Psalms of Ascent. It is not that the life of the one in the City of God hasn't hitherto been blessed; it is just that it has inhabited a different verbal space. Here we have the *esher* variety of blessedness, so to speak.

Though we could do a similar analysis for "fear" in 128:1, I will leap over to the final words of the verse: "who walk in God's way." This is classic "wisdom" or Deuteronomic language. For Proverbs, the best kind of life is where one selects the right "path" or "way." The goal of life is not to turn to right or left from it (Proverbs 4:26-27). Again, the fundamental principal of Torah learning and recitation in Deuteronomy is to do it when you "walk by the way" (Deuteronomy 6:7), which is the same phrase as used in Psalm 128:1. Thus, this Psalm takes us into different realms of speech, though it expresses concepts that are consonant with the steadfastness, satisfaction, joy and fruitfulness we have already seen in the Psalms of Ascent. The presence of Psalm 128, and especially 128:1, teaches us a valuable lesson—that different linguistic universes can easily be accommodated in a robust expression of faith. This Psalm is Exhibit A to make our case. We are on our Stairway to Heaven and we hear the voice of another person on the way, but that person's "accent" and "manner" is different from ours; yet that person is likewise on the way. Life in the City of God is broad enough to accommodate both.

2 "The labor of your hands shall you eat; you shall be blessed and it will be good for you"

The strangeness continues, with the appearance of an infrequently-appearing word for "work" or "labor" (*yegia,* 16x) and a repeated use of *esher.* The double use of "blessed" in this Psalm, as well as its appearance in 127:5, gives us confidence to include this concept into our growing list of things celebrated in Jerusalem: stability, satisfaction, joy, fruitfulness, and *now blessedness.* The one who "speaks a strange language" to us in this Psalm has now given us his gift of language to include in our own expression of faith. We have a five-fold, secure chain of blessings atop the mount. The creed grows, incorporating the experience of those who speak with a strange sound. Though the word "labor" only occurs sixteen times in the Bible, the phrase "labor of your hands" appears in three other places (for those who are inveterate counters, we also have Genesis 31:42; Job 10:3; Haggai 1:11). Deuteronomy 28:33 links the concepts of labor and eating. Thus, we have biblical correspondences to the language used here, also. Psalm 127:2 talked about "eating the bread of pain/sorrow"while here the Psalmist speaks of "eating the fruit of one's hands," with only "eating" being in common. Yet, there is a contrast going on. Psalm 127 talks about the vanity of simply consuming the fruit of one's labor; Psalm 128 speaks of the joyousness of doing that same thing. What is the difference envisioned between the two Psalms? That's for you to answer! Such a person is blessed, and it goes "well" for him/her. By the use of the hyper-common "good" (*tob*), we are back to a widely-shared language of faith. The important point, however, is to notice the role that blessedness now plays for the pilgrim who has climbed the Stairway to Heaven.

3 "Your wife will be a fruitful vine in the inner sanctum of the house; your children will be as the shoots of the olive tree surrounding your table"

The "strange" expression of faith continues, but in a way that is perfectly consonant with the other Psalms of Ascent. We are talking of fruitfulness here, a theme already broached and embraced in Psalm 127. But there it was fruitfulness from 'dad's' perspective; here the fruitfulness is presented from the view of the mother and the children. *She* will be like a fruitful vine; *they* will cluster around the table like olive branches. Combining 127 and 128 gives us a full picture of fruitfulness. Maybe that was the original idea that connected this Psalm to the rest of the Psalms of Ascent in someone's mind in the first place. Vines that bear fruit are a very good thing in a dry land. The mother is like that.

What is fascinating about the language, however, is *where* the wife is. She is in the *yerekah* of the house. This can mean "in the inner part of your house," or "in the sides of your house" or "in the lower story/depths of your house." It is interesting that when Jonah embarked upon the Tarshish-bound ship and became overwhelmingly tired, he went into the *yerekah* of the ship (1:5). Scholars are tongue-tied in trying to determine the meaning of the word, but I have given you three good choices. Some have suggested that this wording might be a sort of forerunner of the "women's quarters," an architectural phenomenon very familiar to those who have visited the Arab/Muslim world. The ancient Chinese had a phrase to describe the women's quarters of a prince's palace—the 闺房 (guilfang2), the women's chambers or boudoir. We don't really know what it means in Psalm 128. Children also will be very important in this fruitful family, gathering around the table as a shoot or branch of olive trees (the word for "shoot" (*shethil*) is a *hapax*, though the verbal form, "to transplant" occurs ten times). I suppose we could call this "blessed fruitfulness," to augment the "fruitfulness" of Psalm 127. As any who have had children can attest, life can't get much more full than when they are gathered round the overflowing table.

4 "Behold, thus shall the man be blessed who fears the Lord"

We continue with "unique to Psalm 128 language," but here it is language that just serves to summarize the pleasant domestic scene painted in verse 3. It is almost that verse 3 has given us a "still life with vines" though "with people thrown in." Would that a contemporary Rembrandt would paint it. In this verse we have a return to the *geber*, the man of the house. The conception of ancient Israel, which isn't too different from the idea of many in our day, is that a husband/father who fears the Lord will be the foundation of a blessed household. A divine pentagram has now been constructed by the Psalms of Ascent; each one of the five corners has a word written: steadfast, satisfied, joyful, fruitful and blessed (in fruitfulness). Life can't get much better.

5-6 "May the Lord bless you from Zion. May you see the goodness of Jerusalem all the days of your life. May you see your children's children. Peace be upon Israel"

When life is going well, we find it relatively easy to be gracious to others or, in the language of this Psalm, to extend "blessings" to others. We have just described the contours of a happy life; now the Psalm concludes with a threefold blessing or three individual blessings (take your pick), blessings that have both societal and familial dimensions. Though the term "happy/blessed" (*esher*) only appears in this Psalm (and 127:5) out of all the Psalms of

Ascent, the related word *barak* ("to bless") appears ten times in the Psalms of Ascent and twice in this Psalm. Because there are more than sixty occurrences of *barak* in the Psalms, its appearance here functions as a sort of "connective tissue" to the rest of the Psalms of Ascent and to the Psalter overall. Blessing is the first and last thought of this little-known Psalm, a Psalm that is growing on us, like the stretching olive vine, with each passing word. Note the parallel structure of the middle two statements. Each begins with the word for "see" ("May you see the good of Jerusalem" and "May you see your children's children"), and each ends with the object of the wish ("good of Jerusalem"/"children's children").

Once you have been in the Heavenly City your most intense longing is that prosperity and blessings continue. Once you have been in the Heavenly City and experienced the fourth of the blessings (fruitfulness), you want that fruitfulness to continue. The phrase "children's children" has a particularly resonant character to it, and is especially reminiscent of the phrase in Psalm 103:17, "But the mercy of the Lord is from everlasting to everlasting upon them that fear Him, and His righteousness unto children's children," a phrase almost identical to that of Psalm 128:6. May the blessings on Israel increase! May the blessings on the pilgrims who are now in the Heavenly City continue! May there be prosperity in homes and joy in families! May this all happen. Hmm. . . Are we tasting heaven a bit too early? The next few Psalms will answer that question. . .

Notes

Psalm 129 A Song of Ascents.

1 "Often have they attacked me from my youth"
  —let Israel now say—
2 "often have they attacked me from my youth,
  yet they have not prevailed against me.
3 The plowers plowed on my back;
  they made their furrows long."
4 The Lord is righteous;
  he has cut the cords of the wicked.
5 May all who hate Zion
  be put to shame and turned backward.
6 Let them be like the grass on the housetops
  that withers before it grows up,
7 with which reapers do not fill their hands
  or binders of sheaves their arms,
8 while those who pass by do not say,
  "The blessing of the Lord be upon you!
  We bless you in the name of the Lord!"

Psalm 129 in a Nutshell

Students of Psalm 129 are unanimous in affirming that this psalm has a communal dimension to it. The exhortation, "Let Israel now say," and the probable references to a national calamity (perhaps the Babylonian exile) in verses 3-4 suggest its fittingness in some kind of celebratory liturgy recalling deliverance from national danger. No doubt. But, in keeping with the theme I have been developing in this book, and consistent with the flow of ideas in this Psalm, I would like to read this psalm as reflecting a new dimension in the spiritual life of those who are "standing within your gates, O Jerusalem" (cf. Psalm 122:2). Seen from this perspective, Psalm 129 gives us a challenging but realistic development of life in the City of God, along the Stairway to Heaven. It is challenging because it suggests that even after the five-fold realization of grace that attends the one who has made pilgrimage (stability, satisfaction, joy, fruitfulness, special blessing), there remain difficulties, difficulties that are reminiscent both of the Psalm 120 life in "Meshech and Kedar," and the problems overcome in Psalms 123, 124. It is realistic because it suggests that even when things are going very well for us, and have been going well for some time, perils may impend.

1-2 "How greatly have they troubled me from my youth, let Israel now say. How greatly have they troubled me from my youth, though they have not prevailed against me"

Both the structure and one word from verses 1-2 are familiar to us from earlier Psalms of Ascent. The twofold repetition of the subject (in this case "how greatly have they troubled me from my youth") is reminiscent of the repetitions at the beginning of Psalm 124 and Psalm 127. Repetition either allows for antiphonal response, if sung in a group, or for fixing a concept deeply in the mind. And the word chosen to reflect abundance or great degree of trouble (adjective is *rab)* is identical to the word from Ps 123:3, 4, describing the abundance or great degree of contempt or scorn directed at the Psalmist from others. A verbal link creates the opportunity for linking of ideas, and we are not mistaken to see the Psalmist possibly returning to the unhealthy part of his journey at the end of Ps 123. As you recall, he was standing in Jerusalem and still contemplating those who had hurt him. In some ways it is like standing at the foot of majestic Everest and complaining that the snow is covering your boots. Yet complaints and difficulties abound even in the Heavenly City.

Though the word "distress" or "vexation" (*tsarar,* a verb that also elsewhere can be translated as "enemies" or "adversaries") that appears twice in succession in verses 1, 2 is not replicated in other Psalms of Ascent, it occupies a similar meaning universe as the *buz* (contempt) of 123:3 and the *laag* (mocking) of 123:4. It also is a frequently-appearing word in the Psalms in general (16 of 52 Biblical appearances are in the Psalms). The most famous or familiar appearance is in Psalm 23:5 where the Psalmist celebrates the Lord's ability to prepare a table for him in the presence "of my enemies" (*tsarar* is word). The word for "prevail" is the frequently-appearing *yakol* ("to have power/be able") and functions similarly to the words "swallow up" and "overwhelm" in Psalm 124:3, 4. Thus, for the author of Psalm 129, enemies are still in his memory, as in Psalm 123, and they haven't overcome him, as also they didn't overcome the author of Psalm 124.

The presence of enemies that continue to stalk a person, even when in Jerusalem or the city of destination, is reminiscent of the sobering concluding lines of John Bunyan's seventeenth century classic *The Pilgrim's Progress.* Christian, Faithful and Ignorance were approaching the Heavenly City, the absolute final stage on their journey of salvation. But just before entry, two shining ones (representing angels), who had conducted Christian and Faithful to the City, took Ignorance, bound him hand and foot, and led him away. Then they carried him through the air to the door, a door that led to hell, that Christian saw on the side of the hill. The angels placed Ignorance there. The most chilling line of *Pilgrim's Progress* follows: "Then I saw that there was a way to hell even from the gate of heaven, as well as from the City of Destruction." Bunyan's sober Puritanism suggested that the life of faith faces potentially fatal perils, even to the end. . . Whatever your reaction to Bunyan's theology, one might agree that Psalm 129:1 recalls the dangers that still exist for one who has felt quite secure in faith for some time. Here the dangers will be of the "stabbing or searing memories" kind.

3 "They carved deeply into my back; they made their furrows very long"

This is one of the most overlooked verses of personal distress in the Scripture. It is here, in this verse, that the Psalmist decides that the "remedy" of Psalm 124 will not be enough for him. That is, five Psalms previously the author also narrated his past troubles, but was content to say that they didn't overwhelm him. Here the Psalmist says the same thing, by saying that "they have not prevailed against me," but then, rather than moving on to a more optimistic topic, *he returns to a narrative of the troubles.* A reversal of spiritual fortune happens when you can't be 'content' with the 'victory' you *know* is yours today, but somehow you have to relive the dangers and wounds of earlier battles. . ..battles that you have *already* won! But by reliving those battles, you wound yourself again. That is what the Psalmist does here, and especially in Psalm 130. The narrative and experience of victory of Psalm 124 isn't enough for him now.

But before we criticize the Psalmist too deeply, we must realize the two-fold nature of memory. Memory is both a most precious gift that shapes our identify and gives us strength, but it also can present the most severe challenges to us. Blessing and bane. It gives us location and solidity in life to be sure, but it also houses the most dangerous paths and potentially noxious byways. In this case, the Psalmist goes deeper into the past memories, and they are gruesomely expressed here. Though the word *gab* can be translated several ways in the Bible, "back" is no doubt the best here. A slightly different word is used for "back", though the same mental world is broached, in a most horrifying verse from one of Isaiah's Servant Songs, "I gave my back (*gev*) to the smiters and my cheeks to those who make my face smooth" (by plucking out the beard)." The combination of deep pain and personal humiliation is behind both verses.

In Psalm 129:3, the Psalmist is likening past humiliations to plows going over his back, carving their blade deeply into his flesh. And, to make things worse, the second half of the verse goes further. The furrows (*maanah*—a rare word whose meaning is fairly certain) are "lengthened" (*arak* occurs 34 times and carries with it the concept of prolongation, either of time or distance). So, not only are the carvings in the back painfully deep, but the furrows, those carvings, are made long. To pick up on the image of the carving being on one's back it would be sort of like having furrows from neck to butt and then back and forth again. That is what the distress felt like, and the Psalmist wants to 'go there' or wants to take us with him there. Sometimes the pain of past abuse is so strong that it can't be 'wished away' by even the skillful use of the most powerful 'victory' vocabulary. The scars of the past are just too deep.

4 "The Lord is righteous and has cut off the cords/ropes of the wicked"

The Psalmist will try to "remedy" his reopening of the old wounds in verse 3 by applying a divine poultice to it in this verse. The words he chooses to describe this are also powerful: "He (The Lord) has cut off the cords." If we connect this thought to the preceding verse, the following picture emerges: the Psalmist recalls the days where his back was turned into a plowed field. The etchings are still deep in his back. But now, the cords tied to the animals that plowed those furrows have been cut (*qatsats* is an infrequently-appearing verb whose meaning is, invariably, to "cut/cut asunder/cut in pieces"). The implication then is that the Psalmist, as he was in Psalm 124, would be "free" from these assaults and then able to resume the stability (Psalm 124:8) of his spiritual life. But, as we read on, it simply doesn't happen that way here.

5 "May all who hate Zion be put to shame, may they be turned back"

Rather than regaining his spiritual center and calmly confessing his renewed trust in the Lord, the Psalmist now chooses to enumerate or wish various kinds of judgment upon the evildoers who had oppressed him. The "evil" or "wicked" people of verse 4, the ones who have carved the furrows into his back in verse 3, need to get their comeuppance; the Psalmist will wish for it in verses 5-8. The images he uses to describe the judgment he wants to attend his enemies may not appear as vivid as plows engraving our backs, but they are nonetheless memorable and equally noxious. They center around three things: shame (v 5), desiccation (vv 6-7), and isolation (v 8). The combination of "put to shame" (*bosh* is verb) and "turned back" (*sug* is the verb) in this verse is, perhaps unsurprisingly, repeated elsewhere in the Psalms. Though Psalm 129 uses two verbs to describe the desired action (*bosh, sug*), four verbs actually swirl around the concept of "turning back and putting to shame" in an earlier Psalm. Psalm 40:14 (also repeated in Psalm 70: 2) gives us the full panoply:

"May those who seek my life be put to shame and confounded/ embarrassed; may those who delight in bringing adversity (to me) be turned back and be dishonored."

This fourfold collection of verbs, then (*bosh, chapher, sug, kalam*—someone, please, come up with a mnemonic!), neatly captures the concepts of shaming, confounding, turning aside, humiliating. That is just what you want for those pesky foes, even if they only are stalking you in your memory.

6-7 "Let them be like the grass on the rooftops which dries up before it can even be plucked up, which will not fill the hands of the reaper or the bosom of the sheaf-gatherer"

After the shame wished on those who hate Zion, on those who have done evil to him, the Psalmist goes on to wish them desiccation. The word "dry up" or "wither" (*yabesh*) is the "Janus-word" here, whose meaning swings both ways in the sentence—dry grass on the roof, dry harvest so small that it can't even be clutched to the bosom. The image is strikingly reminiscent of another "dry" image in the Scriptures, Psalm 11:6, where the author uses the typical word for "rain," but then ironically turns it on its head by wishing the "rain of snares and fiery brimstone" on the wicked. That Psalm concludes, "and a burning heat (of famine) will be their cup of tea. . ." literally 'the portion of their cup.' The brutality of the image in agricultural-oriented cultures is palpable. Upon further reflection on Psalm 129, I think that the image of desiccation may be as cruel as the image of plows carving up the back even though the torture is of a different kind. One is the sharp pain of immediate violation; the other is the lingering distress and then demise of those starving to death.

Taking apart the images one at a time in 129:6-7, we have: (1) rooftop grass that withers before it is "plucked." The word I have translated "plucked" is *shalaph*. In almost all of its twenty-five occurrences, it means "to draw a sword." The most natural reading is grass that withers before it even takes root and grows, but the Psalmist doesn't pick those more common verbs in presenting his image; (2) the emptiness of the "hands and bosom" of those who reap or gather sheaves. That is, the grass is so thin, so dried up, that even those skilled at gathering small portions in the harvest will come back empty-handed. Some of the words are difficult to understand (for example, the word translated "bind sheaves" is a rare-occurring word in Scripture and never, other than possibly here, means "bind sheaves"), but the image of moisture deprivation is clear. The image is particularly fascinating in the context of the Psalms of Ascent. Just three chapters ago the Psalmist was rejoicing as he brought in the sheaves; now he wishes no sheaves on the enemies of Zion.

8 "And passersby don't say, 'The blessing of the Lord be upon you. We bless you in the name of the Lord'"

This is also a chilling ending to the three-fold image of judgment wished on the enemy just discussed. Added to the shame and humiliation of verse 5 and the deprivation of moisture in verses 6-7 is now isolation, characterized by the absence of greeting and fellowship in verse 8. Previous commentators have helped us interpret this verse by pointing us to a parallel in Ruth 2:4 where the daily greeting of those passing by the reapers at their work is given.

> "Boaz came from Bethlehem, and said to the reapers, 'The Lord
> be with you. And they answered him, 'The Lord bless you."

If this was indeed a custom, much like a friendly "hello" or "God be with you" in our day, it is a pleasant one. Mutual wishing of the Lord's blessing adds a tone of serious fellowship and even friendship to encounters that are otherwise seemingly inconsequential and fleeting. But the point of this verse is that, because of the scanty harvest, *no one* says these greetings. Or, better yet, the Psalmist wishes on the enemies a situation where they are greeted by none as they do their fruitless toil. As we conclude two-thirds of the Psalms of Ascent, then, one can be forgiven for asking the question of whether the Psalmist is really in a better place than he was back in Meshech and Kedar of Psalm 120. Certainly, from one perspective, things are better. He has the stability, satisfaction, joy, fruitfulness and blessedness that came through Psalms 124-128. Yet, he has allowed himself to return to memories of past abuse and has responded to those searing memories by wishing a similar kind of punishment, though really a slow torture, on the "enemies" or "evildoers." There may be some satisfaction in wishing evil on the adversaries, but this satisfaction comes at the expense of sacrificing the spiritual stability and even joy of the previous Psalms. As the Psalmist gets "warmed up" here, all words of familial warmth and joy disappear. He descends into the world of judgment and retaliation. Maybe that is inevitable for us. We don't always stay atop the mountain. We want to explore the crevasses in the rock. That is where the Psalmist leaves us at the end of Psalm 129. We had so much hope, and now we are wondering about the nature of this new life in the Heavenly City. What kind of life *is* it? Psalm 130 will deepen our concern even more.

Psalm 129 A Song of Ascents.

Notes

Psalm 130 A Song of Ascents.

1 Out of the depths I cry to you, O Lord.
2 Lord, hear my voice!
Let your ears be attentive
     to the voice of my supplications!
3 If you, O Lord, should mark iniquities,
     Lord, who could stand?
4 But there is forgiveness with you,
     so that you may be revered.
5 I wait for the Lord, my soul waits,
     and in his word I hope;
6 my soul waits for the Lord
     more than those who watch for the morning,
     more than those who watch for the morning.
7 O Israel, hope in the Lord!
     For with the Lord there is steadfast love,
     and with him is great power to redeem.
8 It is he who will redeem Israel
     from all its iniquities.

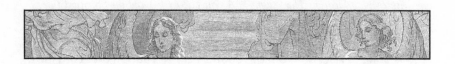

Psalm 130 in a Nutshell

As with its predecessor, so this Psalm can be seen both as a communal and an individual Psalm. Israel as a community no doubt could identify with it and use each of its phrases as an expression of national penitence or lament. Its meaning, however, becomes more powerful for us if we see it in the context of the theory we are developing: that the Psalms of Ascent reflect the yearnings, confessions, delights and hopes of a pilgrim to Jerusalem who is now in the City of God. More specifically, we have seen that the one who had climbed the Stairway to Heaven, who had learned to live a life of stability, satisfaction, joy, fruitfulness and blessedness in Psalms 124-128, had just now descended into the netherworld of his own memories in Psalm 129. At first the memories were seemingly vincible but then, unexpectedly, they turned into an expression of judgment on foes. We ended Psalm 129 with a rare thing: the only place in Scripture where one wishes that a blessing *not* be said over someone else. And that is where Psalm 130 opens. Seen in light of the flow of the Psalms of Ascent, then, Psalm 130 takes on fresh and powerful meaning. It is an expression of faith, to be sure, but an expression of one who has lost his/her center in life, who has found his/her way into the depths of isolation from God, and from that lowest point cries out to God.

1-2 "A Song of Ascent. From the depths I cry to you, O Lord. Lord, hear my voice. May your ears be inclined to my voice of request for favor"

We are not explicitly told that the judgmental words of Psalm 129 led the Psalmist into the deep waters of Psalm 130, but that is a natural inference from the texts themselves. We might ask the question of why a person who has experienced the five-fold blessings enumerated in Psalms 124-128 might find him or herself in the very bathos of isolation here in this Psalm, but that is a mystery too deep to understand. Dante just said it without explaining it, in the opening words of the *Inferno:*

> "Nel mezzo del cammin di nostra vita mi ritrovai per una selva oscura," ("In the middle of our life's way, I found myself in a dark forest").

The broad "middle" of life just might be, for many, the "destruction that stalks at the nonday" (Psalm 91:6). More specifically, we are now two-thirds of the way through the Psalms of Ascent. Perhaps this is a distress that comes upon one in middle or late middle age. Just when you *thought* that freedom would be yours. . .

This is the only Psalm in our collection where I have decided to put the words "Song of Ascent" in my translation of verse 1. The reason for this is that the consecutive words "ascent" and "depths" in Hebrew provide a delicious contrast. It is a Psalm of "going up," but in this Psalm one is doing this "from the depths." Let's climb up. . .to the pit! One would think that with the number of experiences of distress recorded in Scripture that the word describing this one, *maamaqqim* ("depths"), would appear frequently, but it only appears five times. Yet it inhabits a meaning world shared by several other Hebrew words, among them *tehom* and *metsolah,* and the verbal form of the word used here (*amoq*) also takes us to "depths."

The Psalm that seems to be Psalm 130's closest linguistic and ideological neighbor is Psalm 69. Just as we looked at Psalm 91 as a detailed "commentary" on Psalm 121, we might look at Psalm 69 as a reflection on the experiences of Psalms 129 and 130. Our Psalms of Ascents are only brief songs that skim the surface of some very deep subjects; they need the clarification of other word-smiths who have excavated the soul and come up with other words to capture in more detail the beauty and despair of what they have found. Thus, I look at Psalm 130 as a genuine cry of distress from the depths, but one which receives its fuller understanding through Psalm 69. Though a detailed consideration of Psalm 69 is beyond my scope, a brief exposure to 69:2-4 and 14-15 introduces us to some of its rich language, to the echoes of it in Psalm 130 and, surprisingly, to another of our Psalms of Ascent.

69:2-4, "Save me, God, because the waters have come to my very soul. I am drowning in the mire of the depths, and there is no place to stand! I have come to the depths of the waters! The floods overwhelm me! I am exhausted with my crying; my throat is burning. My eyes give out in waiting for my God"

This is a moving cry from one who has been thrown into the life-threatening waters of distress. The contradiction is evident immediately—the waters are submerging him, but his throat is parched or even burning. Water water everywhere but not a drop to drink. Rather than the waters only coming to his "neck," as most translations have it, we have waters submerging the soul, the very root of the person (*nephesh*). Then there is a threefold, and maybe even a fourfold, connection with Psalm 130. Let's start with the most obvious one-- through the word "depths" (*maamaqqim,* as in 130:2), here "in the depths of the waters." Meditating on the searingly painful words of Psalm 69, the author of Psalm 130 finds his own voice. That, too, is where he is—in the depths, the deepest trenches of the ocean bottom. But Psalm 69 doesn't stop there. These depths are described as a place where one cannot "stand" (the common verb *amad*). Rather than simply seeing the horrific experience of the Psalmist as unique to him, we find the same word "stand" used in Psalm 130. "If you, Lord, should count sins, who could stand" (130:3). Our author has so internalized the rhythms of Psalm 69 that he repairs to the precise vocabulary to talk about this precarious position.

Then, there is the double appearance, in Psalms 69 and 130, of the word "hope" or "wait." Psalm 69 says that his eyes are at the point of failing in "waiting" for God. Picking up on that most hopeful, but sometimes frustrating word, Psalm 130 twice uses it (*yachal*) and twice a synonym (*qavah*) in verses 5-8 to describe the long and sometimes seemingly fruitless wait for deliverance. Finally, there is what you might call a "visual echo" of Psalm 69:2 in Psalm 130:3 through the use of the words "mire" and "sin." The rare word in Psalm 69:2 to capture the "mire" is *yaven*, and the word for "sin" in Psalm 130:3 is *avon*. The words even *look and sound* alike: *yaven, avon*. Psalm 69, then, provides the literary spark for our author to record the depths of his despair. And there is more. The verb at the end of 69:2, "the floods *overwhelm*" is the same rather unusual word used in Psalm 124:4 to talk about waters that *threatened* to overwhelm, but which the Lord didn't permit actually to overwhelm (the verb *shataph*). That is, by linking Psalm 130 to Psalm 69, we are deeply ensconced in forbidding regions. By further linking Psalm 69 to Psalm 124, we recognize the consternation of the author of Psalm 130. The depths of Psalm 130 are now depths that overwhelm in Psalm 69, even though the Psalmist was delivered from them in Psalm 124. But our author has entered new and dangerous depths, depths that threaten not just to weaken but to obliterate.

69:14-15, "Deliver me from the mire, and don't let me drown. Let me be delivered from those who hate me and from the depths of the waters. Don't overwhelm me with waves of water! Don't let the deep places swallow me! Don't let the pit shut its mouth over me!"

Psalm 69 here returns to themes broached earlier in 69:2-4. The same rare word for "depths," which overlaps with Psalm 130, is used again. But the overlaps with Psalm 124 are also evident. Interestingly, the author of Psalm 69 changes the word in 69:2 for "mire," using the more common *teet* in verse 14. The despair of the author continues. We are in the thought world of Psalm 130.

Back to Psalm 130.

130:3-4 "If concerning sins you save a record, O Lord, O Lord, who could stand? But, with you is forgiveness so that you will be feared"

The words of Psalm 130 are fresh and powerful but, because we have studied a few of the thoughts of Psalm 69, we have the feeling we are on familiar ground. The "sins" mentioned by our author are unspecified but are described with a most common Hebrew word, *avon*. Surprising at first is the word used to describe the "measuring" or "keeping a record" of the sins. We normally would have expected the word to come from the world of measurement (*madad* is a common-enough word), but we are taken to the world and common word for "keeping, watching, preserving" (*shamar*). The verb *shamar* became the central word in second half of Psalm 121 to describe the Lord's "keeping" activity. The Lord is our keeper and shade; the Lord will keep our life. Here the Psalmist hopes that the Lord doesn't "keep" records of sins because, if God did this, no one could "stand" (the same word in Psalm 69:2). The Scriptures use many words to describe "forgiveness," but the noun here, and its much more frequently-appearing verbal form (*salach*) gets the point across. Isaiah 43:25 expresses the same idea but with fully different words,

"I, I am the one who wipes away your transgressions to the end that I might forgive you, and not remember (your sins)."

The variety of ways to express similar concepts gives us a verbal suppleness and longing for precision to capture in words, if possible, the precise contours of every movement of the human heart.

5-6 "I have waited for the Lord. My soul has waited. I hope in God's word. My soul (watches) for the Lord more than watchers for the morning, more than watchers for the morning."

These verses are key in triggering the Psalmist's emergence from the depths. And, the "key to the key," so to speak, is the movement of life from "waiting" to "hoping." The past tenses of the two appearances of "wait" give the alluring suggestion that the Psalmist, plunged into the mire of his current depths, is now reciting past acts of having "waited" for God perhaps as a way of "triggering" the reality of hope. How does one get into distress, fall into the depths? Each person could write a book on that one. . .but no doubt there was, for the Psalmist, a time of past physical distress, of emotional or military defeat, of temporary estrangement from family or friends or of having committed an act that needed atonement. The time between suffering the consequences of an action, and thereby ending up in the depths, and actually getting out of the distress is a crucial time for the spiritual life. What do you *do* in the moments that stretch out to weeks and even months, moments in which you are "out of sorts" either physically or spiritually? The double use of *qavah* ("wait") in verse 5, but with the addition of "my soul" (word is *nephesh*), lets the reader know that the Psalmist is now aware that the waiting process is long and difficult. "I have waited." "My soul has waited." Seems like a very long time.

Yet, there are dangers in trying to clamber too quickly out of the pits of life, trying to rise to quickly to the surface out of the depths. Using the image of the depths, divers know that trying to come to the surface too quickly after life deep below the surface can give one the bends, a painful and sometimes life-threatening decompression sickness. One only gradually comes to the surface. Theologically speaking, then, one needs to know how to cultivate hope. The author has turned the corner here because he realizes that the movement from waiting to hoping sometimes takes a very long time. But he never tells us explicitly *how* he moved from waiting to hope, but I will venture a suggestion in the last paragraph of this section.

Just as the word "watch" drops out of the second sentence (v 6, that is, there is no verb there—we translators just supply it for your convenience), so the author "skips" the mental process of how he goes from the "I have waited" to "I hope" in verse 5. Something about the waiting process, likened to those who watch all night, has convinced the Psalmist that hope is a good thing, and indeed a very good thing. And this author is not the only one who has learned this truth. Earlier in the Psalms we have, "none of those who wait for You will be ashamed" (25:3). Though many things might be said about lessons learned in the waiting process, or in the process of going from waiting to hope, one important lesson is learning humility. You realize in the depths that you are no longer the lord of your fate or the captain of your soul. Unless someone else "builds the house" (127:1), the author will stay mired in the depths. If one learns to wait and have that waiting transmuted into hope through realization of humility, one has experienced the most precious divine alchemical process.

Using the language of alchemy, God takes as it were the *prima materia* of our weakness and sin, the "lead" of our "deadened" condition, combines it with the transmuting agent (the "philosopher's stone" of divine grace), and produces a new person, stronger than ever, as valuable as the "gold" sought by the alchemists. This, then, is how I read the importance of 130:5-6. The psalmist's optimism begins to rise even as the distress continues.

God is a God of forgiveness; God will "cover" him again for his rather foolish outburst (as I have read it) at the end of Psalm 129. God will root him out of the depths.

And, we sometimes tend to ignore a very crucial phrase in these verses. It is "hope in God's word" that the Psalmist mentions. The hope in God's word may be the trigger that moves him from past experiences of waiting to the reality of a living hope. A quick study of the appearance of the word *yachal* ("hope") in the Scriptures (40 occurrences) yields the striking fact that *yachal's* greatest concentration in any chapter is in Psalm 119 (six times). That long poem, directly preceding our collection, is the Psalm *par excellence* celebrating the Word or the Law of God and (now we know) urging people to "hope" in this word. By the end of verse 6, then, we see that the long night of waiting still continues, but it is a waiting now of one who is convinced that the dawn is coming. Is that a faint pink streak already in the night sky?

7-8 "O Israel, put your hope/trust in the Lord, because with the Lord is mercy and an abundant supply of redemption. And He Himself will redeem Israel from all its sins"

These two verses provide us important spiritual/psychological and linguistic lessons. First, to the former. Once the author has exhorted himself to hope (v 5), he then urges Israel to hope. The verb "hope" (*yachal*, vv 5,7), then, is the link between the individual and the community. A strengthened individual leads to a strengthened community. Note the similarity in spiritual movement between Psalm 130 and Psalm 22, one of the bleakest of the Psalms. Quoted by Christ on the cross because of its apt description of one mocked and abused (22:7-8) and the feeling of being forsaken by God (22:1-2), the Psalm also explores the emotions of deliverance and the result of that deliverance. After praying to be delivered from the threatening enemies and being assured of that deliverance, the Psalmist then says, "I will tell of your name to my brothers and sisters, in the midst of the congregation I will praise you" (22:22). Psalm 130 has this same movement. Once the author is convinced that hoping in God's word will lead to deliverance, he is emboldened to urge the entire Israelite community to place their hope in God.

But the linguistic lessons are no less important. Even as verses 7-8 give us a most welcome communal conclusion to the Psalm they do so with vocabulary that is strikingly new—new, at least, for the Psalms of Ascent. More precisely, these verses begin and end with familiar words and then, as if giving us a delicious sandwich with unknown ingredients, place two words of explosive theological meaning in the middle. The two familiar words are "hope" (v 7) and "sins" (v 8). If God had make a record of *avon* (v 3), no one would be able to stand. Now, in verse 8, God redeems from those same *avon*. But the two words of explosive theological meaning, though common in the Bible, are unique in the Psalms of Ascent. These two words that give the final crescendo of deliverance are "lovingkindness/mercy" (*chesed*) and "redeem/ redemption" (*padah/paduth*). Books have been written on the former concept; the latter, though appearing in diverse Old Testament contexts, is most familiar from Deuteronomy 7:8,

> "It was because the Lord loved you and kept the oath that he
> swore to your ancestors, that the Lord has brought you out with
> a mighty hand, and redeemed you (verb is *padah*) from the house
> of slavery, from the hand of Pharaoh king of Egypt."

Our Psalm thus closes with a wonderful Hallelujah Chorus of hope, hope that is now supercharged with the most powerful theological vocabulary in the author's verbal treasury. And, to add one little grace note to it all, the Psalmist adds that God's mercy is "very abundant" (verb is the common *rabah*). It is the same word used twice in Psalm 123 to describe the "abundance" of contempt that the Psalmist received from his enemies (123:3-4).

But now the "abundance" of Psalm 123 has been drowned out by the "abundance" of God's redemption in Psalm 130. The hope is now charged with a hope in the divine lovingkindness. The Psalmist seems to have learned his lesson as he boldly urges Israel to hope in the Lord. The long dark night is finally over. . .

Notes

Psalm 131 A Song of Ascents. Of David.

1 O Lord, my heart is not lifted up,
    my eyes are not raised too high;
    I do not occupy myself with things
    too great and too marvelous for me.
2 But I have calmed and quieted my soul,
    like a weaned child with its mother;
    my soul is like the weaned child that is with me.
3 O Israel, hope in the Lord
    from this time on and forevermore.

Psalm 131 in a Nutshell

The Psalmist returns to his spiritual center in this Psalm. The pain following his judgmental outburst (129:5-8) and the deep and long period in the depths (130) has given way to this brief gem of a Psalm, a gem celebrating the quiet life of humility and dependence on God. Our movement from 129 to 131 is similar to the theological flow in Psalm 107:23-30. In that section of Scripture, the Psalmist recounts the terrifying experience of being caught in a storm at sea. What started out as a calm journey was followed quickly by a storm, by waves that mounted the sailors to heaven and then plunged them to the depths. Terrified at the storm, they cried to the Lord in their trouble, and he brought them from their distress (v 28). The storm was stilled and the waves were hushed. That text continues, "Then they were glad because they had quiet" (v 30). Quiet. That is what is celebrated here. We see the quiet of thousands of "Madonna and Child" of the Italian Renaissance as the Psalmist curls up here contentedly on the breast of God.

1 "O Lord, not proud is my heart. And not too high are my eyes. And not with matters that are too great or complex for me do I concern myself"

After the experience of being humbled, the Psalmist takes stock of himself in this verse. He uses three "no's," one at the beginning of the three clauses of this verse, which I have tried to bring out in my literal translation. Once a person has put him/herself forward a bit too brazenly, either in word or deed, and has been chastened for it, that person is cautious about how far to extend the self the next time. The threefold "no" signals this caution. The verbs used in first two clauses come from the area of "raising, elevating or being proud." *Gabahh,* translated "proud" here, has a range of meanings extending all the way from Saul's being *higher* (i.e., taller) than others (I Samuel 10:23) to sparks that fly *upward* in the Book of Job (5:7), to the *lofty* place where God is enthroned (Psalm 103:11). A heart too high, as here, suggests a heart that is proud. The same word is used to describe Hezekiah's heart in II Chronicles 32:25 before his humbling.

Now, to the eyes (*ayin*). We recall in Psalm 123 how the raised eyes were a *good thing*, a sign of a person's directing attention to God, expressing one's dependence on God, even though a different verb is used of "raising" the eyes (*nasa*, 123:1). The eager pilgrim, just starting the journey of faith, also lifts eyes to the hills (121:1). Here we have a Psalmist who *won't* raise (the verb for "raise" is the common *rum*) the eyes. So, there are two kinds of "raising eyes" contemplated here, and the difference in the accompanying verbs is a gentle signal to us in what spirit these eyes are "raised." The Psalmist avoids raising the eyes in pride.

But, even more arresting, the Psalmist doesn't occupy the self with things that are too "great and wonderful" for him. What could this mean, since it is the "wonders" of God that are frequently on the lips of the Psalmist (30/71 occurrences of the Hebrew verb for "wonders/doing wonders," *pala,* are in the Psalms)? Why doesn't *this* Psalmist concern himself (literally "walk in") these wonders? The word rendered "wonders" really is quite a supple word. As mentioned, the verb is *pala* and occurs about 70 times in the Bible. But just a review of the various ways it is translated lets us see its suppleness. It is the word to describe miracles (Exodus 34:10) or a special vow (Leviticus 22:21) or something extraordinary (like the plagues the Lord brings—Deuteronomy 28:59), but its meaning in Genesis 18:14 and Deuteronomy 17:8 is where we want to go. In those two passages the word is used in the sense of something "difficult" or "too difficult" for humans. Something becomes too difficult for us for a number of reasons—perhaps the matter isn't clear, we don't have enough information, we are deficient in understanding, we don't have enough strength. Some matters are just too hard for us.

That is what the Psalmist is saying here. He has realized, through his "dark night of the soul," especially in Psalm 130, that some matters are just too "difficult" for him. Some roads are not healthy for him to go down. We know that is true for us. The twenty-first century phrase, "I don't go there" is a popular way of capturing the meaning. After experiencing distress or trouble, people say, "I won't go there again." That is what it is for the Psalmist. He is saying he won't "go there"—into places that lead him from God or into personal danger. In his particular case, the dangerous place was indulging in thoughts and words of judgment on other people. Maturity in faith and life emerges when you understand which things are "too wonderful" for you, things too difficult which you *shouldn't* explore. It is a mark of humility and self-understanding, rather than lack of intellectual or spiritual confidence, to know your limits.

2 "Certainly I have re-set my soul and quieted it just like a weaned child. My soul is like a weaned child"

We depart from the familiar language of the other Psalms of Ascent in this verse, but the result is a marvelous picture of domestic bliss, comfort and security. The two verbs at the beginning of the verse (*shavah,* 30 occurrences and *damam,*21 occurrences) carry one meaning—that of quieting or settling down. The basic meaning of *shavah* is to "resemble"something or "put/place" something. Perhaps the closest parallel to *shavah's* usage here is in Psalm 16:8, where the Psalmist always "sets/puts" (*shavah*) the Lord before himself. Literally, then, in Psalm 131:2, we have the Psalmist "setting" or "placing" his soul. One might think of it, perhaps, in the phrase we often use in our day— about "re-setting" something to give us a fresh start. Colloquially speaking, then, the soul needs a "re-set" here, especially after the frightful experience in Psalm 130.

But when that soul is "re-set," it is done so through quietness or silence (*damam*). The second verb of 131:2 is *damam.* Though the verb *damam* is almost always translated as "be silent," its most memorable appearance is in Joshua 10:12, where the sun "stands still." The author of Psalm 131 is quiet because he is content and doesn't move. The verb *gamal,* translated here as "to wean/ to be weaned," also has an impressive range of meaning, with "wean" being the right pick for this context. The Psalmist is real- izing the truth of an earlier Psalm—that a day in God's courts is better than a thousand elsewhere (Psalm 84:10). Contentment reigns--and probably not a little gratitude. When you have been extricated from the pit, from the miry slough, from the depths, you both have a new humility towards life as well as a deep well of gratitude. 'I am not going to that place again' is your solemn vow. 'I am re-setting my life. What I am going to do is to settle in to the comfort, rest, quiet and security that is good for me. I will not go to the places that are 'too wonderful' for me.' Getting to this level of maturity and satisfaction is remarkable and heart- ening. It urges us, too, to find that place of quiet "re-set," where we, too, can be like the weaned child. We all need it.

3 "Hope, O Israel, in the Lord from now on, forever and ever"

The verse is identical in thought and in wording to the first words of Psalm 130:7. And, one is probably on the right track to see in this exhortation for Israel to hope in the Lord an invitation to readers of all times and places so to hope. This then would complete the concentric circles of faith—from individual, to nation, to world. Let's pray that prayer of hope in the Lord. Soon we will be singing it (Psalms 145-150).

Notes

_____

_____

_____

_____

_____

_____

_____

_____

_____

_____

_____

_____

_____

_____

_____

_____

_____

_____

_____

_____

_____

_____

_____

Psalm 132 A Song of Ascents.

1 O Lord, remember in David's favor
    all the hardships he endured;
2 how he swore to the Lord
    and vowed to the Mighty One of Jacob,
3 'I will not enter my house
    or get into my bed;
4 I will not give sleep to my eyes
    or slumber to my eyelids,
5 until I find a place for the Lord,
    a dwelling-place for the Mighty One of Jacob.'
6 We heard of it in Ephrathah;
    we found it in the fields of Jaar.
7 'Let us go to his dwelling-place;
    let us worship at his footstool.'
8 Rise up, O Lord, and go to your resting-place,
    you and the ark of your might.
9 Let your priests be clothed with righteousness,
    and let your faithful shout for joy.
10 For your servant David's sake
    do not turn away the face of your anointed one.
11 The Lord swore to David a sure oath
    from which he will not turn back:
    'One of the sons of your body
    I will set on your throne.
12 If your sons keep my covenant

and my decrees that I shall teach them,
 their sons also, for evermore,
 shall sit on your throne.'
13 For the Lord has chosen Zion;
 he has desired it for his habitation:
14 'This is my resting-place for ever;
 here I will reside, for I have desired it.
15 I will abundantly bless its provisions;
 I will satisfy its poor with bread.
16 Its priests I will clothe with salvation,
 and its faithful will shout for joy.
17 There I will cause a horn to sprout up for David;
 I have prepared a lamp for my anointed one.
18 His enemies I will clothe with disgrace,
 but on him, his crown will gleam.'

Psalm 132 in a Nutshell

This is a psalm of communal memory. Various modern English translations divide this Psalm into five (NRSV) or four (NASB) subsections, but I think it is best divided into three parts, centering on what one might call the final movement of the spiritual life as presented in the Psalms of Ascent. This is the movement towards unity—unity of the people of God. Even though one might have companions along the way as one climbs to Jerusalem, it is a profoundly individual journey. *Each person* must make sure that his/her feet don't slip. Then, upon arrival in the City of God, the Heavenly City, we spoke about *individual* memories that stabbed or blessed. Yet beginning in Psalm 132 we have another theme that counterbalances the individualism of earlier Psalms of Ascent. Unity of the people of God will be explored here and in the next psalm but for now we can say that the worship of the people and its liturgy of celebration in Psalm 132 sets in motion the great prayer for unity of the people in Psalm 133. Psalm 132, then, establishes the preconditions for unity. Given that idea, we divide the Psalm into three sections: 1) a common memory (1-5), 2) a common reenacted journey (6-10); and 3) a common confession (11-18). Let's explore each of these themes through a verse-by-verse exposition.

1 "Remember, O Lord, to David's credit all the times he was humbled"

Before reflecting briefly on the role of memory in faith, a word on my translation of the final word here: "humbled" (*anah*). Almost all commentaries render this word as David's "afflictions," and there is good reason to do so. The word *anah* occurs 83 times in the Bible, nearly one-fifth of which are in the Psalms, and in every other Psalmic occurrence it can best be rendered "hurt" or "affliction." "Before I was troubled/afflicted I went astray, but now have I kept your word" (Psalm 119:67). But the word *anah* has a larger lexical field than just "afflicted." It can mean "to weaken" or "humble" or "oppress" or "be busy or occupied" with something. The predominant meaning outside of the Psalms and especially in Leviticus-Deuteronomy is "to humble," as in Deuteronomy 8:16, "and (I) fed you in the wilderness with manna that your ancestors did not know, to humble you (*anah*) and to test you, and in the end to do you good."

The meaning of "humble" for *anah* here makes especially good sense because of humility's role in reconstructing the Psalmist's psyche in the preceding Psalm. After being delivered from the mighty distress of Psalm 130, the Psalmist was in a humble and contrite frame of mind in 131. A humble person recognizes acts of humility in others, and so our Psalmist recognizes that in David's life in 132:1. We don't have to torture ourselves trying to find times in David's life when he might have been "afflicted" or "humbled" in order to make sense of this passage. The Psalmist is doing a "sympathetic reading of history" and almost any adversity faced by David might fall under the category of "humbling."

But the real movement of this verse, and of the entire Psalm, is in the realm of memory. Memory has a purely intellectual component—the recalling and reinterpreting of what is recalled—but it also has what one might call a communal reenactment component. This Psalm celebrates the latter. The Psalmist is not calling on his compatriots and himself to remember past acts of divine greatness, which is a frequent preoccupation of Scripture writers;

he is asking *God* to remember David. Such a desire for God to recall things isn't unknown in Scripture, both in the Psalms (106:4) and, especially, in Nehemiah (5:19; 13:14). The sense of the verse is as I have rendered it: "Credit it to David." The Hebrew only asks God to "remember. . .to/for David," but I think the "credit" translation doesn't stretch things too far. What really is happening in this Psalm is a twofold flow of memory—from God to the people and the people back to God. And the people's remembrance of God is aided by a kind of historical reenactment that will take place in verses 6-10. It is as if every true Israelite is a lifetime member of their equivalent of the Society for Creative Anachronism or the local Civil War Reenactment Chapter.

Psalm 132's placement near the end of the Psalms of Ascent provides us both instruction and hope. It instructs us by highlighting the role that communal memory as well as communal reenactment plays for the people of God. Christians have always believed that the celebration of the Lord's Supper is the principal act of communal reenactment in the community of faith. Thus, it is easy to understand how Israel reenacted its faith, in this case by some kind of "ark ceremony" mentioned in verses 6-10. But it also gives us hope for it shows us that the basis of our new life in the City of God is one celebrated along with the people of God. Our individual pilgrimage has value, indeed great value. But now that this individuality has been celebrated in pilgrimage, it is supplemented by the communal dimension of faith. Once one has truly caught one's "bearings" in the City of God, one truly understands the role of communal memory and celebration among the people of God.

2-5 "When he swore to the Lord, vowing to the Mighty One of Jacob, 'If I come into my own tent, if I climb into my own comfortable bed, if I give my eyes sleep and my eyelids slumber before I find a place for the Lord, a resting place for the Mighty One of Jacob, then. . .'"

I have translated the three *im's* here with the force they almost always have in the Bible—"If." So, David is making a vow. 'If something doesn't happen. . .then let me suffer the consequences.' That is the nature of a Scriptural vow. And the Scriptures are quite clear as to the importance of fulfilling the vow one utters. Leviticus 27 devotes an entire chapter to the issue. Of course we have the example of vows uttered too rashly, as in the case of Jephthah (Judges 11), but a vow served as a kind of solemn asseveration that one would do all in one's power to accomplish what one vowed. It would be quite in character for David to have made such a vow as indicated here, even though the actual words of it aren't found in the historical books. Perhaps by asking God to remember to David's "credit" in verse 1, the Psalmist is trying to "soften" the uncompromising nature of the vow to build the house. 'At least credit to David his dedication, his focus, his incredible drive in the effort to build the house. He aimed very high, and built a kingdom in the process, though the actual construction fell to Solomon.' That is how it *really* happened.

The vow here is stated in perfect poetic parallelism: "come into house/clamber into comfortable bed; give sleep to my eyes, slumber to my eyelids." More precisely, David uses a "double word" for bed in verse 3. Each of the words (*eres* and *yatsua*) is separately (and infrequently) attested in the Scriptures as a "bed" but the two words never occur together outside of this passage. I have rendered it as "comfortable"—as if David is emphasizing the stark contrast between his bed and the lack of a "resting place" for the Lord. It is as if he is saying, 'Every night I climb into a comfy bed and sleep well but You, O Lord, remain unhoused, protected by the flimsiest of tents. How unfitting is *that*!'

The unfulfilled vow of David is a reminder to us that the ambitious person is always longing to do, and sometimes vowing to accomplish, more than can be done. Yet, along the way, s/he may leave remarkable monuments of human dedication, skill and focus. David vowed to build the house, but it didn't happen. He "only" built the kingdom. Note that the conclusion of the vow remains unsaid in the Psalm. We can use our imagination to fill in what isn't said. In one other vow, the Psalmist was clear: "Let my right hand wither, if I do not set Jerusalem above my highest joy" (Psalm 137:5); we can imagine a like fate that David envisioned for himself if his vow wasn't performed.

Many comments on individual words could be made, but only one or two will suffice. God is twice called here "the Mighty One of Jacob." It is a rare appellation, only occurring four times outside of this Psalm (once it is "the Mighty One of Israel"). Its anchor appearance is in Jacob's great valedictory poem of Genesis 49, and this title appears in one of the most stunningly suggestive verses of that amazing poem (49:25). "His hands (Judah's) were made strong through the Mighty One (*abir*) of Jacob." The word *abir*, expressing the concept of mightiness, is only used in this form in the expression "Mighty One of Jacob." Normally, the concept of might is expressed through the identically-sounding *abbir* (17 occurrences). Perhaps David used this specific title for God in making this vow so that he would be linking himself back to the deepest roots of his people and calling on the God who made them strong in that situation. Only one other word needs to be mentioned, and this time on a lighter note. The word for "eyelids" is *aphaph*. We can almost see the eyelids fluttering and then closing time after time—even the word repeats the movement—*aph aph*.

6-7 "Behold, we have heard (the vow, the humility) all the way in Ephrath, we have found it in the field of the forest. 'Let's go to that dwelling place, let's worship at his footstool'"

We are now in vivid historical reenactment mode. The people of God, having taken the Stairway to Heaven and settled into the Holy City, are now plunged deeply into the mystic chords of memory. They are reenacting the moment when their ancestors heard the news of the vow of David and decided that they had to hustle off to the dwelling place of God to see the great things that were going to happen. The news reached from town to forest, its echo reverberated far and wide. 'Hear ye, hear ye! King David has just vowed to build a house for the Lord! Hear ye, hear ye!' The words to describe all these things are pretty common, except for the word "footstool." Yet, because we don't know all the furniture configurations of ancient Israel, we don't know if this was a common or rare piece of equipment. The (Latin) Vulgate translates the word differently in several of its six different occurrences. The meaning is clear—everyone wanted to be part of this great vow, to see how it would actually unfold.

8-10 "Rise, O Lord, to your resting place, you and the ark of your strength. May your priests be invested with righteousness and may your holy ones shout for joy. For the sake of David your servant, don't turn your face from your anointed one."

The historical reenactment continues. Perhaps there was a ceremony where a (fake) ark was carried atop poles and brought into the sacred precincts, as a way of commemorating the bringing of the ark into the temple at its completion years previously. Perhaps two things are being conflated here—the memory of the journey to see this great vow of David fulfilled and the memory of an actual bringing in of the ark (under Solomon). In any case, historical events that happened in fairly quick succession in the distant past can often become conflated into one event in the minds of later people. Note how the language to describe God's "home" changes in the Psalm. David has his own "tent (*ohel*) of his house" (*beth*, v 2) and would no doubt want to build such a "house" for God. But when that house is mentioned, it is a *mishkan*, a dwelling place or tabernacle (v 5). But now, on further reflection, that house becomes a "resting place" (*menuchah*, v 8). The Bible also knows other words for the temple, but these three are helpful in suggesting that there was still no place for God.

Different words reflect the 'verbal discomfort' with not having a divine resting place.

But now, in verses 9-10, the scene shifts; we are in the Holy City, the focus is now on the priests and the accoutrements of worship. That is the goal of pilgrimage, the goal of bringing the ark to the Holy City—that the people of God would worship. And that worship is expressed in an alluring parallelism: the priests are "clothed/invested" with righteousness and the "holy ones" shout for joy. Note the personalization of the concept of being clothed with righteousness in Isaiah 61:10,

> "I will greatly rejoice in the Lord, my whole being shall exult in
> my God; for he has clothed me with the garments of salvation,
> he has covered me with the robe of righteousness."

Isaiah 61:10 uses two of the same words that appear in Psalm 132:9. The section closes with a fervent wish—that the God who preserved and protected David will also not "turn his face" away from his anointed. The terms are fraught with deep historical and theological meaning. "Turn one's face" is a frequently-occurring phrase to describe divine rejection. Note the more eloquent way of saying it in Psalm 104:29, "When you hide your face, they are dismayed/troubled." And, the "anointed" one (the *mashiach*), refer-ring here to the king, was a term that could be used to describe the high priest (Leviticus 6:22) or the one set aside by God to rule (I Samuel 24:10) or, especially, to David and his progeny (Psalm 18:50). We have now completed the historical reenactment, from past to the current day. The ark has been brought up to the temple. All are standing around in anticipation of what is to come.

11 "The Lord has sworn to David and will not turn back from it: 'I will place on your throne one of the fruit of your body'"

Now is the time for common confession of the people of God (verses 11-18), a recitation of their fundamental beliefs. Yet, unexpectedly, that confession is here put primarily in the mouth of God. Over the next several verses God will affirm the divine commitment to Israel, to the house of David, to this particular place in the earth. Thus this Psalm closes with a paean both to a particular place and the broad diversity of the people of God. God, the Lord of all the earth, has chosen to place the divine name in this particular place. And God will establish and fight for that name. Just as David swore to build the house (for which the Psalmist wants God to "give him credit"), so the Lord is now swearing (same word) His commitment to providing for the future of the people. The purpose of celebrating memory is to assure a secure future. The past provides strength, location, rootage in order to welcome the future. And that future will be with one of the children of David on the throne.

12 "If your children keep my covenant and the testimony I will teach them, then you will not lack a son for ever to sit upon your throne"

Ah, the catch. Just as David uttered his vow and then backed down slightly (for Solomon actually built the house), so the Lord gently qualifies the oath in verse 11. There has to be obedience—that is the fundamental principle for continuation of the covenant. The Scriptures present us with an unresolved tension—is the continuation of Israel's existence dependent on Israel's obedience or solely on the divine promise of an eternal kingdom? We should give a tentative "yes" in answer to the question and move on. . .

13-18 "For the Lord has chosen Zion; He has strongly coveted it for his dwelling place. 'This will be my resting place forever and ever. I will dwell right here, because I have greatly desired it. I will certainly bless the people with yield of the hunt/provisions; the poor I will satisfy with bread. I will clothe the priests with salvation and the holy ones will shout with unmatched joy. There I will also cause to bud/sprout a horn for David, I will stretch out the lamp for my anointed one. Yet the enemies I will clothe with shame, but on him (the king) will blossom/ sparkle his crown'"

I have provided a few different translation options above to make more clear, if possible, the parallel constructions and diverse word choices in Hebrew. Let me list a few of them. The priests are clothed with salvation, but the enemies are clothed (same word) with shame. Salvation (*yesha*) and righteousness (*tsedeq*, a characteristic of the priest's garments in verse 9) are the opposite of shame (*bosh*). What a great way to build vocabulary!

Two similar-meaning verbs are given for things that will grow up or sprout—the horn of David and the crown. Thus, we have *tsamach* (usually referring to plants that spring up) and *tsuts* (a synonym to describe the flourishing of plants), an euphonious alliterative combination that again makes learning vocabulary a joy. In addition, we have a fourth word now used to describe a dwelling or divine dwelling—we have already seen "tent of a house" (v 3) and "dwelling place" (vv 5,7) and "resting place" (v 8), but here we have a "habitation" (*moshab*, v 13).

But what is most unexpected about these verses is the appearance of highly-charged emotional language to capture the divine pleasure in and human reaction to Jerusalem and, specifically, the divine "house." Three pairs of words should be noted. The first is "desire/greatly desire" (*avah*, vv 13, 14). Only appearing 25 times in the Bible, the verb *avah* covers the linguistic waterfront from "greedy" (Numbers 11:34) to "covet" (Deuteronomy 5:21) to "have a craving for (II Samuel 23:15) to "greatly desire" (II Samuel 3:21 and frequently). Here we have a God who eagerly longs for

Jerusalem, who desires it, who craves it as the divine place to settle down. We see that the emotion felt by the people of God is reflected in the divine response. Second is the repeated *barak*, "to bless" in verse 15. God will greatly bless, and not simply "singly bless," the poor of the earth. This is a theme not developed in the other Psalms of Ascent but invites deeper consideration—but not in this book! Finally, the twofold *ranan* (a shout for joy or ringing cry, v 16) of God's *chasid(im)* or holy ones makes this more than a ringing cry of joy; it is a sign of unmatched exultation. Everyone it seems, except for the enemies who will be put to shame, is engaged in this celebrative event in Zion. God wants to be there; the people reenact that joy; all groups rejoice in it; the future is assured. With this strong declaration of communal faith, echoed by God's faith in the people and the place, all that is left for the community of faith is to celebrate their unity—which is the theme of Psalm 133.

Psalm 132 A Song of Ascents.

Notes

Psalm 133 A Song of Ascents.

1 How very good and pleasant it is
    when kindred live together in unity!
2 It is like the precious oil on the head,
    running down upon the beard,
    on the beard of Aaron,
    running down over the collar of his robes.
3 It is like the dew of Hermon,
    which falls on the mountains of Zion.
    For there the Lord ordained his blessing,
    life forevermore.

Psalm 133 in a Nutshell

The last great movement in the symphonic richness of the Psalms of Ascent is from humility to unity, a unity that is captured in Psalm 133. The Psalmist experienced the former of these during the long night of waiting in Psalm 130, and then spoke about it in Psalm 131. This then led to a movement of unity in Psalm 132, where the *recalling* of David's vow, the *reenactment* of ark-delivery to Jerusalem and the *reaffirmation* of God's promises to Israel took place. It was as if, to use a Deuteronomic approach to life, all Israel "stood there" before the Lord, recognizing its dependence on God and God's promise to them. But then, after doing this, after lifting eyes to the one enthroned above the cherubim, lifting eyes beyond the hills to the God who gives protection to the city, eyes settle back down to one's surroundings, and it dawns on one anew that one is celebrating these things not alone but with representatives of the whole people of God. One says, 'Yes, this is not only *my* God but *our* God, and thus those who are standing next to me are my kindred in the faith and in the fight, my kindred for now and for evermore. And you think, 'How wonderful it is for kin to be standing here together, in unity, in celebration, in common life!' *That* is the tone of Psalm 133.

1 "Lo, how good it is, and how pleasant, for brethren to dwell in togetherness"

This verse bristles with theological plenitude. What looks like two very common, nondescript and even secular terms (*tov* and *naiym,* "good" and "pleasant") take on special meaning when we realize that these are combined a few Psalms later (135:3) and connected with the special pleasures and joys of worship.

> "Praise the Lord, for He/It is good *(tov).* Sing his name for It/He is pleasant *(naiym).*

The good thing envisioned in Psalm 135:3 is either God or the praise of God. The lack of a pronoun leaves the precise meaning unclear. The pleasant thing is either God's name or to sing to God's name. Armed with this insight, we might be tempted to return to Psalm 133 and see it in the context of the declaration of Psalm 135. Praise is good, God is good; the name of God is pleasant, God is pleasant; "good and pleasant" take us then on a journey soaring back to the God who made us. Though we certainly will affirm the goodness and pleasantness of the unity at the end of the verse, we pause and realize that the first two words are quintessential words of theological affirmation.

"Give thanks to the Lord, for God is good" *(tov,* Ps. 136:1); "in your right hand are pleasant things forever" *(naiym* are the "pleasant things," Ps 16:11). The two words have such a powerful and favorable connotation. But the really good thing, according to this verse, is for "brethren" to "dwell" "together/together in unity." Each of these three Hebrew words requires the briefest comment. Some scholars take the word "brethren" (literally "brothers," *achim*) as pointing only to the extended family. The meaning then would be, "How great it is when all my extended family lives near me." I suppose we would all agree that this is a pleasant thought, especially if you get along with all your second cousins, but I believe the Psalmist is playing for higher stakes here than simply family harmony. In this case I read the word *achim* as it is used in Psalm 22,"I will recount your name to my brothers *(achim)*, in the midst of the congregation I will praise you." That it, "brothers" is in parallelism with "congregation:" it means the same thing.

It is good when the congregation of Israel "dwells together." The word for "dwells" is the usual one, *yashab,* occurring more than 1000 times in the Bible, but when put in the context of the "quest for a divine home" in Psalm 132, it takes on new meaning. God has finally found a home, after many years and four different words (in Psalm 132); now the people of Israel dwell together. And they dwell *yachad.* The word is also a frequently-occurring one, and its most vivid use for me is in the moving narrative of Genesis 22, where Abraham and Isaac trudge on "together" (the word is used twice—vv 6, 8) as they go to the venue of sacrifice. "Together," then brings a note of intimate interconnection, both of physical and psychological proximity. Thus, this verse flows with the pleasant theme of the congregation dwelling together near the "dwelling" place of God, celebrating the close connection in worship and life. The next verse deals with other things that "flow."

2-3a "It is like oil, the good oil, which runs down the head onto the beard, the beard of Aaron, which then runs down to the collar of his robe. It is like the dew of Mount Hermon, which runs down upon the hills of Zion"

Before expositing this verse, I did a quick internet search on "images or pictures of unity" in cyberspace. In almost all cases one has people or icons, with hands joined or embracing, celebrating some aspect of their common life. The icons, or the people, are almost always in a circle. So, imagine my initial surprise when realizing that the image of unity in 133:2 is flowing oil (v 2) or flowing dew (v 3). It is not the usual thing that comes to mind when someone says, 'Draw unity, please!'

Scholars have racked their brains to come up with reasons why these two rather arresting and visually-alluring images are associated with the togetherness of the people of God described in verse 1. Three theories surface, the third of which is most appealing to me. Some suggest that it is the *fragrance* of the oil and the dew that is like the *fragrance* of unity, but that seems to be a real stretch. Others talk about the *abundance* of the flow of oil; the high priest (represented by Aaron here) is the only one of the priests who has scented and well-mixed oil *poured* over him (Leviticus 8); the other priests are *sprinkled* with oil. And, as for the dew on Mount Hermon, travelers for ages have commented on its abundance. But, again, that would lead us to think something like this: the oil and dew are abundant; the people are in abundance in Jerusalem; the joy and fellowship is abundant. This is not as much as a stretch as the first theory, but it is hardly a point that merits the beautiful images.

Rather, I note the three-fold presence of the verb "flow down" or "go down/descend" (*yarad*) in these verses. I think it is something in the *movement* or *flow* of the oil or dew that is the reason for the analogy. I note in passing the interesting coincidence that the same verb is also used three times in Jonah 1 to describe the "downward" movement of Jonah as he is fleeing the presence of God (down to Joppa, down to the ship, down to the bowels of the ship). In our Psalm, however, that downward movement is "redeemed" by the realization that both the oil and the dew are flowing down as it were "from God" or "from above." The oil flows down, first to the beard and then to the opening of the neck hole of the robe. The little word *peh* in verse 2 is the same word used repeatedly in Exodus 28:31-32 to describe the "neck hole" of the high priest's robe.

Some have even interpreted the word to mean "fringes" of the high priest's robe. In any case, it is oil of consecration, starting as it were from the hand of God and flowing down the head and beard of the high priest. And the dew, though the result of a natural process, is repeatedly connected in Scripture with its divine source. For example, in his poetic blessing of Jacob, Isaac wishes that God would give him the "dew of heaven, and the fatness of the earth, and plenty of grain and wine" (*tal* is the word for "dew," Genesis 27:28, 39). Interestingly, the word for the "fatness" of the earth is *mashman,* obviously related to the word for oil (*shemen)* in 133:1. Perhaps the author of Psalm 133 is connecting the unlikely pair of oil and dew in 133:1 because of the deep, and perhaps even unconscious, effect of the poetic tradition, reflected in Genesis 27:28, on him.

But one can say more. When the manna fell from heaven on the Israelites, it was seen first as a kind of "dew from heaven" (Exodus 16:13, 14— *tal* is used in each verse). Seen in this light, then, the dew that flows and the oil that flows are both indications of the gifts flowing down from God to the people of God. Unity, then, is like the oil, like the dew—it is a precious gift from the Mighty One of Jacob. Note, too, that the same word (*tov,* "good") is used to describe the quality of the oil in verse 2 as well as the "goodness" of the unity in verse 1. Every time one sees the re-enactment of the anointing of a high priest, or one even sees the dew on Hermon, one is reminded of unity.

And, the Psalmist takes one more little step in this verse. It is the dew of Hermon that "flows down" to the hills or mountains of Zion. All agree that nature doesn't *really* work that way. There is no supernatural conduit to take the dampness of faraway Hermon and deposit it on the mountains around Jerusalem. But the fact that dew appears outside of Jerusalem also has probably encouraged the Psalmist to see that transfer process as if in his own dream. Therefore, the Israelites have a daily reminder, in the dew on the nearby hills, of the unity of the people of God. It is a most precious unity, one that needs to be preserved at all costs.

The dew or oil *descending* in the penultimate Psalm of Ascent is a fitting complement to the eyes *ascending* in the second Psalm of this collection, Psalm 121. It is as if the gaze going up to God is met by the dew and oil coming down from God. The glance is full of expectant longing; the oil and dew is the antiphonal divine blessing.

3b "For there it is that the Lord has commanded a blessing. It is life everlasting"

This half-verse brings us back to reality. Rather than soaring with the Psalmist in the dreamy world where dew from Hermon mysteriously waters the hills around Jerusalem, we are brought back to the fact of place and blessing. The word *sham,* "there," refers to Jerusalem, the place that God has put His house for no other reason than that He has desired it (132: 13-14). That is where the person who has made the pilgrimage is directed, back to Jerusalem. A few chapters later the Psalmist will say even more vividly, "Let my tongue cleave to the roof of my mouth, if I don't remember (her), if I don't make Jerusalem rise above my highest joy" (137:6). It is to Jerusalem that memories will be directed. And this memory leads to "life for evermore/life everlasting." If we read this promise also in connection with an earlier Psalm, it takes on a powerful meaning: "For with you is the fountain of life" (36:10, same word as "life" as in 133:3). Thus our last thought is of coursing oil, flowing dew, cascading fountains of dew, and all of it leads to life—forever. When you have this combination, you are just about finished climbing the Stairway to Heaven.

Notes

Psalm 134 A Song of Ascents.

1 Come, bless the Lord, all you servants of the Lord,
　　who stand by night in the house of the Lord!
2 Lift up your hands to the holy place,
　　and bless the Lord.
3 May the Lord, maker of heaven and earth,
　　bless you from Zion.

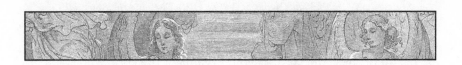

Psalm 134 in a Nutshell

This, the second-shortest of the Psalms of Ascent, is a fitting vale-diction to our long and mostly-pleasant journey. We started in the lands of Meshech and Kedar and now we end in the heart of Jerusalem, in the temple precincts. Night has fallen, the day's work is completed and, before going off to their places, the pil-grims utter a final blessing on those whose work seems to be the most drudging—the night watchers in the temple. The Levites were given charge of security and administration of the temple and its grounds. Vigilance needed to be maintained not simply during the daylight hours, when people congregated, but all night long. No sacrifices or vow-making took place in these night hours. There is only a simple, quiet hush enveloping the environs as the long watches of the night seemingly stretch out to eternity. Breaking that silence are the antiphonal words of this Psalm. The pilgrims utter verses 1-2; the night watchers say verse 3.

1 "Lo, there, bless the Lord, all you servants of the Lord, who stand in the house of the Lord in the night"

Psalms 133 and 134 start at the same place: *hinneh*, "behold" or "lo" or "look." The online New English translation renders it "Attention!" It is a word that directs people to something very important to follow—either the unity of the people of God or, in this case, the task of continually uttering blessings to God. We know from that least-read section of one of the least-read portions of Scripture that certain groups of Levites were "responsible for the work (of the temple) day and night" (I Chronicles 9:33). This is part of the continual 24/7/365 prayer and praise cycle, a human symphony of care that tries to be faithful in response to the care God has shown the people. We don't know until the final word of this verse that we are at night (i.e., the last word of the verse is *layelah*, "night"). But the night watchers of the temple have a no less important, though less visible, role to play as those who place their hands over the sacrificial animals before slaying them. Our newly-arrived pilgrims encourage them in their long and some-times seemingly unrewarding task. Keep up your work, and may God's blessing attend you! That is the tone of it.

2 "Lift your hands, holy/holiness, and bless the Lord"

It is somewhat ironic, but not at all unfitting, that these final words uttered by the those who made the journey present us with a translation problem. We know all the words; we just don't know how best to translate them. My translation is a literal one; the word *qodesh* (from the root *qadash*, "to be set apart/consecrated") gives us problems. It is a noun, usually translated "sacredness/ holiness." Most translators solve the problem by saying that it means "sanctuary," because that is the "holy place." But it really means "sacredness" or "holiness" or the adjectival forms of these words ("sacred/holy"). It can't really rendered "sacred hands" or "holy hands" because we would have expected a plural form of the adjective though, it must be admitted, Biblical Hebrew grammar can at times be quite uncertain. Yet if it is "sanctuary" (i.e., "holy place"), we don't know if the Levites are to lift hands "in" the holy place or "to/towards" the holy place or even "in holiness" as if it were describing a posture or attitude. There is no preposition before the word "holy/holiness," which usually is necessary if you want to translate it "to the holy" or "in the holy."

Upon second thought, when you are unwrapping the Christmas presents you really aren't concerned if the wrapping paper comes from Filene's or Jordan Marsh. So, though a lot depends on a red wheelbarrow for poet William Carlos Williams, not much depends on our translation choice here. One can render it as I have translated it above, and thereby distribute the meaning of "holiness/holy" to both clauses of the sentence. If one wants a Scriptural parallel to this thought, the best one might be Psalm 28:2, "Hear the voice of my supplication, as I cry out to you, as I lift my hands towards your holy sanctuary." Lifting hands, as well lying in a prone position, is the sign of a suppliant; the Levites play that role at night on behalf of the people of God before God.

3 "(May) the Lord bless you from Zion, the Lord who made heaven and earth"

Elsewhere in Scripture, we are informed that God's blessing comes from Zion. "Out of Zion, the perfection of beauty, God shines forth" (Psalm 50:2). This memorable verse from Psalm 50 uses an even more memorable alliteration: *yophi Elohim hophea,* "beauty God shines forth." We can just imagine the glints of beauty turning into a meteoric shower of light coming forth from Zion. We often lose *so much* in translation. . . The Lord who made heaven and earth at the beginning of time (same phrase in Genesis 1:1) is the same Lord who will bless today. The Lord who made heaven and earth (same phrase) at the beginning of *our* journey (Psalm 121:2) is the same Lord who will bless today. The Lord who made heaven and earth (same phrase as in Psalm 124:8), who brought us out of initial distress in the Holy City and removed threatening obstacles is the same Lord who will bless us today. What more can you really say other than to wish that the Lord, who made heaven and earth, continues the blessings?

Notes

CPSIA information can be obtained
at www.ICGtesting.com
Printed in the USA
BVHW031214040720
582859BV00002B/17